The Integration of Mental Health Social Work and the NHS

To order, please contact our distributor: BEBC Distribution, Albion Close, Parkstone, Poole, BH12 3LL. Telephone: 0845 230 9000, email: **learningmatters@bebc.co.uk**.

You can also find more information on each of these titles and our other learning resources at **www.learningmatters.co.uk**.

The Integration of Mental Health Social Work and the NHS

DAISY BOGG

Series Editor: Keith Brown

LearningMatters

First published in 2008 by Learning Matters Ltd

British Library Cataloguing in Publication Data
A CIP record for this book is available from the British Library

ISBN: 978 1 84445 150 0

Cover and text design by Code 5 Design Associates Ltd
Project Management by Swales and Willis Ltd
Typeset by RefineCatch Limited, Bungay, Suffolk
Printed and bound in Great Britain by TJ International, Padstow, Cornwall

Learning Matters Ltd
33 Southernhay East
Exeter EX1 1NX
Tel: 01392 215560
info@learningmatters.co.uk
www.learningmatters.co.uk

FSC
Mixed Sources
Product group from well-managed
forests and other controlled sources
Cert no. SGS-COC-2482
www.fsc.org
© 1996 Forest Stewardship Council

Contents

List of figures

Foreword to the Post-Qualifying Social Work Practice series

All the texts in the Post-Qualifying Social Work Practice series have been written by people with a passion for excellence in social work practice. They are primarily written for social workers who are undertaking post-qualifying social work awards, but will also be useful to any social worker who wants to consider up-to-date practice issues.

The books in this series are also of value to social work students as they are written to inform, inspire and develop social work practice.

Keith Brown
Series Editor
Centre for Post-Qualifying Social Work, Bournemouth

About the author

Daisy Bogg has worked within the social care field for the past 15 years, within mental health and addiction services, for both integrated statutory sector and partnership voluntary sector organisations. She currently holds the post of Consultant in Mental Health Social Care for Bedfordshire and Luton Partnership NHS Trust. Her current portfolio includes approved social work services, safeguarding adults, Mental Capacity Act and a range of social care practice development and governance responsibilities.

Daisy lives in the east of England with her husband and her cat.

Acknowledgements

A debt of thanks is due to so many people for making this book possible. I am going to try and include as many of you as possible, but if I miss you out please don't take it personally!

Firstly, a huge thank you to my husband, Terry, who is not only a contributor to this text, but who also painstakingly sorted out my truly terrible grammar, made lots of tea, and let me neglect him in the last few weeks of writing, without moaning too much.

Thanks to Luke and Di, the editors involved in this project, for having faith that I could actually do it and for dealing with my increasing panic and erratic work submissions. Thanks are also due to my PA, Jan, for generally just knowing what I need to hear when I need to hear it, and also to Fay Brown, for being both a seriously good social worker and a seriously good manager – a rare combination in my experience.

Many moons ago, when I first moved from working in the voluntary sector and into statutory social work, there was one man who kept me both focused and supported. He taught me what being a social worker is actually about, and has had a huge part to play in both my career to date and the experiences that led me to the point of writing this book. His name is Chris Aylott, and without him I think I would have probably given up and gone back to pulling pints for a living many years ago!

Thanks are also due to some of the people who were willing to share their experiences, wisdom and comments with me: these include Claire Barcham, John Watson and Wendy Paskell.

Thanks to Dr Mehraj Shah and Dr Akeem Sule, two medical colleagues who contributed to this book, and who were willing to spend time and effort in finding out and presenting the doctor's view of the whole integration agenda.

Finally, a huge thank you is due to the many service users I have had the privilege of working with over the years – you know who you are! Being involved in someone's life, to the extent that social workers often are, can be both a frustrating and a rewarding experience, and each of you has taught me a valuable lesson about who I am, both as an individual and as a professional . . . these experiences are ones which should never be underestimated, and are the very reason that social work should never be just a job – it truly is a vocation, and one which I am proud to follow!

Introduction

The integration of services has now been high on the agenda for nearly a decade, and some regions are further along the path than others. With this in mind the purpose of this book is to explore the issues from a social care perspective.

The following questions will be addressed throughout this text:

- Is the NHS able adequately to manage local authority duties?

- How do issues such as Approved Social Work provision fit in?

- Is the independent and autonomous social work role at risk?

- Can a social approach really be adopted within health?

- What do we have to learn from the experience so far?

Nationally, NHS Trusts and local authorities have differed in their interpretation of and approach to the arrangements, and this book aims to examine the experiences so far.

While it is recognised that the integration agenda has definite impacts upon health care delivery and perspectives, this text is written from a social care perspective and is part of the Post-Qualifying Social Work series. With this being the case the PQ framework and National Occupational standards for social work are aligned to each chapter, the aim being to provide a useful resource and source of reflection for social work professionals operating within health-dominated and integrated delivery frameworks with mental health service users.

The overall aim of integrating health and social care provision is to improve the experience of the service user, and achieve 'seamless services'. The 2006 joint health and social care white paper *Our Health, Our Care, Our Say* reinforced this position, and seeks to locate the service user and user-led outcomes as central to the care delivery process. The aim throughout this text is to explore a number of aspects relating to these policy directions: for example, does integration mean seamless, and what are the effects of integrating social services and health environments and cultures?

The clash between medically driven and socially driven approaches has long been discussed among social science commentators and academics. With this in mind this book will seek to establish whether these two approaches have now been reconciled, or whether the reality of modern service provision continues to create a range of power struggles and demoralisation among the professional groups.

The principle of integrated, seamless, person-centred care is not contested by any profession. However, the different agendas, perspectives and issues, such as resources, alongside the professional power struggles, all make the task a difficult one. From a social work perspective, our profession has long been seen as the poor cousin. While the introduction of protection of title, professional registration and agreed codes of practice have enhanced the position, whether this has been enough, especially given the lack of definition of what social work actually is, is still a live and contested issue. Within a large and institutional organisation such as the NHS, which has its own power hierarchy, traditions, practice and cultures, how do the social care and social work perspective and principles compete, and can the two cultures ever be truly integrated?

Chapter synopsis

A range of aspects of integrated care services is discussed and debated throughout this text. There are many significant factors within the agenda that have an impact upon social work and social care, especially when considering where these perspectives fit within the NHS culture and services.

Chapter 1 seeks to provide an overall context to the integration agenda, upon which the rest of this text will rest. A range of perspectives and areas will be discussed throughout this book, and the central framework of coordinated services is the context in which all these discussions will occur.

Chapter 2 will build upon the legislative context already presented, examining the policy framework and considering implementation and implications of the modernisation agenda, within which integration is central.

Chapter 3 examines the social work professional identity within the context of a multi-professional capability structure, and Chapter 4 explores the theoretical perspective – asking whether there is a middle ground between the social and medical models of mental health and mental health care.

Chapters 5, 6 and 7 consider partnership and the models of service delivery that have been adopted by health and social care organisations across the UK in order to deliver the integrated care agenda.

This discussion is continued in Chapter 8 where financial arrangements are specifically considered as a fundamental aspect of care delivery.

Chapters 9–12 consider a range of specific groups, and invites comments from other disciplines to consider the impact of integration on the wider sector, and finally Chapter 13 brings all these discussions together and explores the overall issue of what have been the benefits and consequences of integration across the broad spectrum of areas, and what has been learnt by the experience.

By considering all these perspectives and areas associated with the integration of health and social care within mental health service provision, it is hoped that a balanced dialogue and debate can be achieved, whereby social workers entering into such an arena, or undertaking post-qualification awards within the field, will be able to consider their experiences within a whole-system view, and social work as a profession will be able to contribute to the further development of integrated services from a balanced and informed position.

This book is an important step in terms of promoting the social work voice within mental health service development, as it is considered that social workers have a potentially key role to play in the modernisation of services. The following discussions take the stance that as professionals who are well versed and experienced in the newly established value bases and competency frameworks, social workers have the potential to lead and guide health colleagues in understanding the nature of holistic person-centred care. With this being the case, it is as important as it ever has been for social work professionals to articulate and promote their perspectives, roles and functions in order to be participatory and credible partners with their health colleagues in the delivery of high quality, outcome-focused mental health care.

Chapter 1

Setting the scene – the past, the present and possible futures

To know an object is to lead it through the context that the world provides.
(William James, American philosopher and psychologist, 1842–1910)

PQ framework

Achieving Post-Qualifying Social Work awards

This chapter will assist in the meeting of National Occupational Standards for Social Work:

Key Role 5, Unit 15: Contribute to the management of resources and services.
Key Role 6, Unit 18: Research, analyse, evaluate, and use current knowledge of best social work practice.

For registered social workers considering or working towards post-qualifying awards, this chapter will also assist in meeting the requirements of both the specialist award in mental health, and the national occupational standards in mental health which are core to the post-qualification standards in this area.

MHNOS 81: Sustain and review collaborative working.
MHNOS 86: Monitor, evaluate and improve inter-agency services for addressing mental health needs.

PQ Specialist Award in Mental Health:

47 (iv) The legal and policy context of mental health including awareness of relevant local, as well as national, policy contexts.

Introduction

Over the past decade the emphasis on joint health and social care provision within the field of mental health care has been a significant policy direction. Traditionally, social care and mental health services have had a significant overlap; however, towards the end of the 1990s there was an increasing awareness of the lack of collaboration and cooperation between providers, which was resulting in both gaps and overlap in services.

Following on from the implementation of care in the community, which was formalised by the NHS and Community Care Act 1990, attention was being focused upon the delivery of care services. Many teams were already considering the co-location of staff, and multi-disciplinary mental health teams had begun to be the norm in terms of delivery of community services.

Despite these shifts there was still a demarcation between the role of the community psychiatric nurses (CPN) and medical staff, and the role of social care. While teams were beginning to form and there was an increase in cooperation, the improvement in terms of service delivery was minimal and very much focused on either health needs or social needs, rather than a real awareness of a whole-person approach to all the needs a person may present.

Care in the community represented a large shift in how mental health services were delivered and perceived by both professionals and the public. For over a century asylums and large hospital-based campus accommodation had been the preferred method of care. Medical treatment, with a focus on medication and containment, had been the usual practice, and the closure of hospitals and emphasis on community-based provision signalled the first shift towards a more needs-led service. For social workers within the field this was the first time that the government agenda had truly considered a more value-based social welfare model, and social services departments became major players in the transformation of care for individuals experiencing mental distress.

The National Service Framework for Mental Health (NSFMH) and the development of the Care Programme Approach (CPA) were, and still are, significant in terms of the policy direction of integrated care; however, the Health Act 1999 was the legislation that sought to formalise the notion of 'seamless' services into a reality.

From CPA to the Health Act 1999

Following the introduction of community-based treatment, the introduction of the care programme approach (CPA) was the first significant attempt to coordinate care management across the disciplines within mental health services. The aim was to streamline the assessment and treatment planning systems, and to enable a single process that followed the service user throughout his or her journey through the myriad of care services. Introduced in 1991 (DoH, 1991), the CPA system has been referred to as the cornerstone of government strategy in the mental health field, and formed the first stage of the modernisation agenda for health and social care services that is still in existence today.

The NSF, published in 1998, built upon previous developments, and sought to provide a strategic overview and direction to the service improvement initiative that the CPA process had begun. The focus of the NSF was to ensure that coordinated services that were 'safe, sound and supportive' were developed across the country (a full discussion of the policy framework is provided in Chapter 2).

Over the next five years the focus of developments in mental health services was placed upon coordination and collaboration between health and social care providers, in order to prepare for and implement the aims of the NSF. At this point there was little in terms of legislation to support the modernisation agenda. As a result health and social care, while attempting to cooperate, were finding it difficult to reconcile the various statutory duties and requirements.

The Health Act passed through parliament in 1999, and implementation began in 2000. This piece of legislation was designed to allow organisations to formalise partnership arrangements in terms of service delivery under section 31, in formal agreements described as the 'Health Act flexibilities'. These flexibilities allowed local authorities, PCTs and NHS Trusts to enter into arrangements that formally delegated operational duties which had previously been statutory duties confined to a specific organisation. Figure 1.1 provides further details on the areas covered by the flexibilities.

These arrangements signified the first real statutory move to recognise overlap, and the need for coordination. The policy statement issued by the Integrated Care Network – a body associated with Care Services Improvement Partnership (CSIP) and the Department of Health – stated:

> *The statutory bodies do not give up their ultimate responsibility for the functions, and will want to monitor the partnership arrangements. The partnership arrangements are permissive powers that enable closer coordination of services so that services are improved, and outcomes for users can be bettered.* (Integrated Care Network, 2006)

In the case of mental health services it appeared that in most instances the NHS, and most commonly partnership trusts, became the lead agency for the delivery of services.

A range of agreements was entered into by the involved partners that enabled the joining-up of the delivery of health and social care services in the community setting. Community Mental Health Teams (CMHT) were the first area of mental healthcare to be coordinated, and the Health Act flexibilities allowed the transfer of duties, such as the Community Care assessments and procurement of social care services across the professions within a multi-disciplinary setting. This transfer of duties, while remaining accountable to the parent organisation, meant

Figure 1.1: Health Act flexibilities

Pooled budgets:
Allowed health and local authorities to bring resources together into a single pot, accessible to all partners to commission and provide services.

Lead commissioning:
One authority is able to delegate functions, and transfer funding, to the other to take responsibility and manage a single budget for commissioning both health and local authority services that meet the strategic needs of all partners.

Integrated provision arrangements:
Makes it possible to provide health and local authority services from within a single service provider, through a delegation of functions.

that the host organisation entered into a new regulatory relationship with the social services inspectorate, and later the Commission for Social Care Inspectorate (CSCI). This has resulted in a new set of performance indicators that need to be evidenced against team activity. As a result, local authority performance ratings became directly dependent upon the perform-ance of their partner organisations, and partnership management boards were established to monitor the performance of organisations against the agreements made under section 31.

Section 31 – Contract or commissioning arrangement?

While the purpose of applying the Health Act flexibilities is viewed overall as a positive step, the practice of delivering these arrangements has been somewhat more complex. Many partnership trusts have found themselves in an uncertain position, being both partner and provider within the local health and social care economies. This duality in nature can be difficult to manage, and the success of the partnership arrangements is dependent upon both the relationships between partner agencies and the quality and specificity of the original, and any subsequent, section 31 agreements.

Section 31 of the Health Act 1999 states:

> *31 (1) . . . enabling prescribed NHS bodies (on the one hand) and prescribed local authorities (on the other) to enter into prescribed arrangements in relation to the exercise of –*
>
> *(a) prescribed functions of the NHS bodies, and*
>
> *(b) prescribed health-related functions of the local authorities,*
>
> *if the arrangements are likely to lead to an improvement in the way in which those functions are exercised.*

Section 75 of the National Health Service Act 2006, which supersedes section 31, uses the same terminology and maintains the flexibilities defined in the 1999 Act.

The level of prescription attached to these arrangements has been variable across the coun-try, with some areas clearly stating performance indicators, and other areas opting for a more general overview of what is to be delivered, and by whom. In some areas the applica-tion of the legal framework was viewed as 'heavy handed' (Glasby and Peck, 2003), espe-cially where pre-existing partnership working arrangements were in place. In other areas there was a clear reluctance to enter into formal agreements (Glasby and Peck, 2003; Balloch and Taylor, 2001), and a significant overhaul of operational services was required to ensure that organisations were 'fit for purpose' to take on the partnership agenda. The NHS Plan (2000) continued the emphasis on partnership, and financial incentives were introduced to encourage organisations to take on the partnership agenda and enter into formal joint-working arrangements. Throughout these developments there remained a discrepancy across the country in terms of the application of the flexibilities. This situation is still present within many partnership organisations, and in some cases agencies are finding themselves on 'shifting sand' as arrangements are in the form not of formal contracts or commissioning arrangements, but of a set of strategic aims.

Such circumstances have the potential to leave provider services open to criticism from their partners, which is based on political and financial pressures rather than actual performance. This is especially the case as new policy and legislative requirements are introduced, which were not accounted for in the original partnership arrangements.

The impact of a changing regulatory framework

With the inception of partnership arrangements between health and social care came awareness that the regulatory frameworks that governed each sector needed to be aligned. The health service is mainly regulated and inspected by the Health Care Commission (HCC) in the form of core standards, and social care by the CSCI, in the form of social care standards and the performance assessment framework (PAF). Each framework has a number of requirements, and in the case of partnership organisations both are potentially applied to the services. Figure 1.2 provides a sample of the different standards (HCC and CSCI)against which such organisations are assessed.

In addition to the above standards, the Mental Health Act Commission (MHAC) and a range of risk assurance requirements are placed upon NHS partnership trusts. These include clinical governance standards, via the National Institute of Clinical Excellence. With each of these frameworks of standards in place, partnerships can find themselves in a situation of competing regulations, and the centralised strategic direction, via the Department of Health, is to combine the HCC, CSCI and MHAC into a single regulatory body.

Currently, the core and CSCI standards have separate emphases, one of which is on service delivery and the other on service users. Each framework specifies a range of indicators in order to assist organisations to provide evidence of their compliance, and to create an inspection criterion which can be objectively applied. This principle was further supported by the 2006 joint health and social care white paper *Our Health, Our Care, Our Say*, which

Figure 1.2: Current inspection standards

Core standards	CSCI standards
Safety of patients	Improved health and well-being
Clinical effectiveness and cost effectiveness	Improved quality of life
Governance	Choice and control
Patient focus	Freedom from discrimination/harassment
Accessible and responsive care	Economic well-being
The care environment and amenities	Personal dignity
Public health	Making a positive contribution

commits to a single outcome framework, against which all health and social care services can be assessed and governed.

The Department of Health is currently in the process of developing an accountability framework which aligns the different structures, with the aim of a phased implementation between 2008 and 2011. The consultation stage of this development has now closed, and a number of proposals have been made, which include:

- strategic objectives linked into three areas – better health and well-being; better value for all; better care;

- a set of 40 outcomes and indicators aligned to the strategic areas to cover the whole range of health and social care outcomes.

This proposed framework represents a key reform within the provision of services, and has the potential to reinforce the integration of health and social care by bringing together the governance requirements which have traditionally been segregated. In addition, such a move has the potential to assist partnership organisations to create shared goals, one of the key elements that has previously been lacking within the arrangements.

Social inclusion and the personalisation agenda

A range of developments and agendas has been developed within the social care field over the past five years: these include issues such as social inclusion, wellbeing and self-direction of care. Mental health is a key area within these agendas, as it has long been recognised that the social context of an individual has a significant impact upon mental wellness.

Personalisation of care is not a new concept within the social perspective, and is consistent with the core social work values.

In 2007 a ministerial concordant entitled *Putting People First: A Shared Vision and Commitment to the Transformation of Adult Social Care* was agreed across a range of health and social care departments. The signatories included the NHS, the Local Authority Confederation, the Department for Work and Pensions and CSCI. This agreement set out a number of values that bodies committed to, in terms of the development of individualised and social inclusive services. These aims are set out in Figure 1.3. Cross-sector initiatives, such as promotion of individualised budgets and direct payments, along with supporting user-led local organisations and the development of workforce strategies, are all indicated as means by which these shared aims can be achieved.

This shared vision is one of the foci of the developing accountability framework, and is consistent with both health and social care professional values, as it makes the service user central to the provision of services.

Overall the future regulation of integrated health and social care services appears positive, with a commitment on both sides to improving service provision and aligning and coordinating two sectors that have traditionally been on either sides of a divide in order to provide high quality care and support for those who need it.

Figure 1.3: Putting people first – ministerial concordant agreed aims

All services delivered will focus on:
- Living independently
- Staying healthy and recovering quickly from illness
- Exercising maximum control over their own lives and lives of family members, where appropriate
- Sustaining a family unit which avoids children being required to take on inappropriate caring roles
- Participating as active citizens, both economically and socially
- Having the best possible quality of life, irrespective of illness or disability
- Retaining maximum dignity and respect

Transforming Social Care and New Ways of Working

Two further agendas that need to be considered in terms of the delivery of health and social care services are *Transforming Social Care* (DoH, 2008) and *Mental Health: New Ways of Working* (DoH, 2007a). These two areas are set to have a significant future impact upon the delivery of services.

New Ways of Working was originally introduced to look at the modernisation of the psychiatry role; however, as the project progressed it was expanded to encompass other professions. From a social work perspective four key areas were identified:

1. Identity

2. Research

3. Career Progression

4. Leadership. (DoH, 2007a)

These areas are consistent with the professional development and post-qualifying emphasis within social work. The focus on evidence-based practice and the centrally defined competency frameworks have helped social care to assert its unique perspective and contribution, and thus promoted the approach within the multi-disciplinary environment.

Transforming Social Care, a new initiative announced in February 2008, is the policy steer which is directing the development of social care services. The emphasis in this case is moving away from the professional roles that *New Ways of Working* is attempting to define and develop, and towards user-led assessment, with professionals acting as advocates and brokers rather than experts delivering care.

How mental health services are going to deliver these two agendas has yet to be determined; however, discussion and debate are required from the early stages of implementation. The integration of health and social care services has further challenges ahead and social care is a significant partner and player in defining and shaping the direction of travel.

This chapter has sought to provide an initial understanding of the context, which will be further developed throughout this text. The social care perspective is a significant voice within the integration agenda, and one which has traditionally placed the service user perspective at the centre of its overall ethos. This text explores the ranges of issues and challenges that have arisen over the last decade and attempts to place the social model of mental distress central to the debate.

Further reading

Glasby, J. and Peck, E. (2003) *Care Trusts: Partnership Working in Action*. Abingdon: Radcliffe.

Health Act 1999

Chapter 2

Government direction: a policy framework

It was once said that the moral test of government is how that government treats those who are in the shadows of life – the sick, the needy and the handicapped.
(Hubert H. Humphrey, 1911–1978, US Vice-President)

PQ framework

Achieving Post-Qualifying Social Work awards

This chapter will assist in the meeting of National Occupational Standards for Social Work:

Key Role 5, Unit 17: Work within multi-disciplinary and multi-organisational teams, networks and systems.

Key Role 6, Unit 18: Research, analyse, evaluate and use current knowledge of best social work practice.

For registered social workers considering, or working towards post-qualifying awards, this chapter will also assist in meeting the requirements of both the specialist award in mental health, and the national occupational standards in mental health which are core to the post-qualification standards in this area.

MHNOS 81: Sustain and review collaborative working.

MHNOS 86: Monitor, evaluate and improve inter-agency services for addressing mental health needs.

PQ Specialist Award in Mental Health:

47 (ii) Applying knowledge, understanding and skill in relevant legal and policy frameworks.

47 (x) Utilising and applying knowledge and research from other disciplines.

Introduction

The past ten years have seen extensive work from central government in terms of reform of mental health strategy, and the emphasis has changed dramatically from containment and management, to independence and well-being. Although this shift in emphasis began in the 1950s, it has taken many years to embed the principles within policy that can be translated into front line service delivery.

There have been three significant policy agendas over the past decades that have directly influenced the shape of current mental health services. These are modernisation, social inclusion and well-being, all three of which are linked together and wholly consistent with social work core values. The legislative framework, discussed in Chapter 1, has supported these agendas, and this chapter seeks to outline each of these and consider the implications for social work as a profession.

Modernisation agenda

In 1998 the government published a white paper entitled *Modernising Mental Health Services: Safe, Sound And Supportive* (DoH, 1998a), the overall aim of which was to outline the vision of what mental health services should look like. The development of the care programme approach over previous years (DoH, 1990; 1991; 1999a), alongside the two white papers *A First Class Service: Quality in the New NHS* (DoH, 1998b) and *Modernising Social Services* (DoH 1998c), had foreshadowed the vision and subsequent reform of mental health service delivery, and had started the process of coordinated and effective care provision across both services and disciplines.

The ethos of the white paper was threefold: it recognised that both protection and care were at times required for the patient and the community, and that this should be provided in a safe, sound and supportive manner.

Safe: to protect the public and provide effective care for those with mental illness at the time they need it;

Sound: to ensure that patients and service users have access to the full range of services which they need;

Supportive: to working with patients and service users, their families and carers to build healthier communities. (DoH, 1998a)

From a social care perspective these aims have traditionally been at the core of the value base. Social workers are skilled at assessing the two conflicting elements of care and control. The Approved Social Work role in particular requires assessment competence that considers both the risks and the rights associated with the patient and their presenting condition.

Reflection point

When considering risk and personal rights within your practice, what elements inform the decisions and actions that you take?

The introduction of the National Service Framework

The National Service Framework (NSF) for Mental Health was published in 1999, and drew on the principles of the previous white paper. It set out the standards that were required based on ten guiding principles. These were developed by an External Reference Group, chaired by Professor Graham Thornicroft from the Institute of Psychiatry, and were as follows:

- to involve service users and their carers in planning and delivery of care

- to deliver high quality treatment and care which is effective and acceptable

- to be well suited to those who use the services and non-discriminatory

- to be accessible so that help can be obtained when and where it is needed

- to promote the service users' safety and that of their carers, staff and the wider public

- to offer choices which promote independence

- to be well coordinated between all staff and agencies

- to deliver continuity of care for as long as this is needed

- to empower and support staff

- to be properly accountable to the public, service users and carers.

(DoH, 1999b)

With these underpinning values, the NSF set out seven standards that were designed to improve service delivery and hence contribute to improving the mental health of the nation. The standards targeted service delivery across the different tiers of provision, from primary care to acute inpatient and specialist teams, with the overall aim of creating effective provision and care pathways. The aim was to facilitate the service user's journey through services depending on the level of need he or she presents with at any given time. These areas are defined in the NSF as follows:

- Standard 1:   Mental health promotion

- Standard 2:   Primary care

- Standard 3:   Access to treatment

- Standard 4:   Effective services

- Standard 5:   Effective services away from home

- Standard 6:   Carers

- Standard 7:   Prevention of suicide

From a social care perspective this was a welcome development. The holistic and far-reaching scope of mental health issues has been on the social work agenda for many years. The training that is provided for professional social workers (including Approved Social Work training) considers the whole range of psychosocial impacts upon an individual. The introduction of the NSF is highly complementary to the social work profession, as it aligns an individual and community's needs with appropriate interventions. This can vary from prevention and education, through to acute admission, and considers aspects such as carer roles, family dynamics and equality issues, all of which have the potential adversely to affect mental health conditions.

Systems, the NSF and the social care perspective

The social care perspective is essentially systems-based, although it draws on a range of approaches and theoretical bases. The central premise is that the individual's level of functioning is dependent upon the relationships and interactions between the various individuals/communities and the environment. The underpinning values espoused by the NSF serve to inform the actions within each standard and place the service user as the central focus throughout, a premise that is wholly consistent with the social care perspective and with social work as a profession. Figure 2.1 illustrates the potential systems involved within an individual's experience of mental health issues and the provision of care.

As this illustration demonstrates, there are many factors that can influence an individual's experience of mental health difficulties. Each of these factors has the potential to interact with the others, to either compound or ease the levels of distress the person experiences. The NSF represents central government's attempt to recognise the whole range of issues and create 'seamless' service provision that is comprehensive enough to aid individuals in myriad ways, whether they are just at the start of their contact with services or more chronic consumers of mental health provisions. The emphasis on an individual's journey is a positive

Figure 2.1: Systems within the service user experience

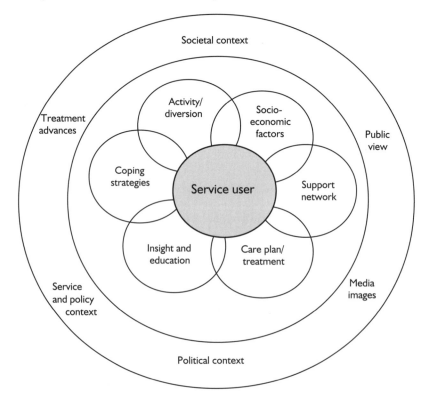

step within development and improvement agendas, as it is a recognition that recovery from mental health problems is both a possibility and an aim: the service users can exit as well as enter services as their needs fluctuate.

Reflection point

At what point do you consider exit strategies for service users you work with?

Taking the NSF standards individually, each has a value and contribution to make to improving service delivery. The combination of delivery of all the standards within a whole system of care assists the potential for positive outcomes for the users of services.

Figure 2.2: Case study example – Mr W

Mr W is a 52-year-old Asian man who presents to his GP with anxiety and depression; he has been experiencing these symptoms since his marriage broke down approximately two years ago. Mr W has been isolating himself from his friends and has stopped going to work. Mr W has two children, one of whom lives in the same street and provides him with practical support. His GP has started a course of anti-depressants and provided him with a sick-note; he has also referred him to the CMHT for support and treatment.

NSF-related Care Plan:

Mental health promotion (Standard 1)
Psychoeducation is offered to Mr W to assist him in identifying situations which raise his anxiety and act as triggers to deterioration of his mental health.

Primary care (Standard 2)
Mr W's GP is able to provide basic services and act as a signposting agent to facilitate maintenance of his mental health on a day-to-day basis.

Access to treatment (Standard 3)
The GP is aware of secondary services and is able to identify and make the appropriate referrals due to agreed care pathways that aid access to treatment for individuals.

Effective services (Standard 4)
Following assessment within the CMHT by a nurse and a social worker, Mr W is offered talking therapies and a psychosocial treatment programme to accompany his medication regime, both of which are supported by a proven evidence base and NICE guidelines for his particular condition and needs.

Effective services away from home (Standard 5)
Mr W does not require admission at this time; however, should he need this in the future the CMHT team is supported by the crisis resolution team, which could facilitate access to a short-term crisis bed if respite is required or inpatient admission if his condition deteriorates to the point where this is needed.

Carers (Standard 6)
Mr W's daughter is offered a carer's assessment and if her needs require it, support services to ensure that the caring relationship is maximised and supported by services wherever possible.

Prevention of suicide (Standard 7)
Mr W has no history of suicidal ideation or self-harm; however, he is still assessed within this area and provided with an agreed crisis and contingency plan if he should experience such thoughts.

This demonstrates that the NSF standards have the potential to provide a whole-systems approach to the presenting difficulties of any given service user on a micro-level. On a macro-level the standards can be applied to national and regional targets to provide consistency in provision and ensure that evidence-based practice is applied across services.

In 2004 Louis Appleby, National Director for Mental Health (also termed as the Mental Health Tsar), published a review of the implementation progress of the NSF (Appleby, 2004). This report indicated that much activity had been undertaken in relation to implementing the NSF, but that over the following five years substantial work was still required. In particular, attention is required in the area of social exclusion of people with mental health problems in order to reduce stigma and discrimination and improve employment prospects.

Social inclusion

The social exclusion unit (SEU) was established in the late 1990s as a response to the growing awareness that vulnerable groups' ability to take part in and contribute to society was not equitable. There was also an increasing concern regarding the range of discrimination that individuals faced when attempting to access mainstream services. The creation of the Social Exclusion Unit (SEU) was in part recognition 'that a cross–government approach to improving the life chances of the most disadvantaged in our society' (Social Exclusion Taskforce, 2007) was required. The SEU has since been superseded by the Social Exclusion Taskforce (SET) which sits within the cabinet office and continues the research and strategy work that was commenced by the SEU in this area.

One of the key concerns in relation to the mental health service user group was the recognition that recovery from mental health problems was far reaching and included socio-economic influences such as access to work, housing and the benefit system. This recognition led to a directive from central government for services to consider the wider psychosocial impacts within an individual's treatment plan, and to expand the care planning process beyond medical management of current presenting symptoms. This led to the widespread application of the social inclusion agenda within mental health services.

Social inclusion agenda within mental health services

In 2003 the government commissioned a report from the SEU to examine the level of social exclusion experienced by people with mental health problems, and recommend a plan for action. This report was published in 2004 and coincided with review of the NSF. It set out a 27-point action plan to bring together the work of government departments and other organisations, recognising that exclusion in mental health terms was a wide-ranging issue that required coordination and cooperation if any real progress was to be made. The overall aim of this report was to improve opportunities and outcomes. The action plan was categorised into six key areas for attention:

1. Stigma and discrimination

Challenging negative attitudes and promoting people's rights;

2. The role of health and social care in tackling social exclusion

Implementing evidence-based practice in vocational services and enabling reintegration into the community;

3. Employment

Giving people with mental health problems a real chance of sustained paid work reflecting their skills and experience;

4. Supporting families and community participation

Enabling people to lead fulfilling lives the way they choose;

5. Getting the basics right

Giving access to decent homes, financial advice and transport;

6. Making it happen

Setting out clear arrangements for leading the programme and maintaining momentum. (SEU, 2004)

These areas are aligned with the standards within the NSF for Mental Health, and also continue the pattern of reflecting social care and social welfare principles within development of strategy and service provision. From the inception of social work professional training, the task of challenging discrimination wherever possible has been a core value (CCETSW, 1989). As such the profession should be encouraged by work such as this, which reflects the tasks and values that are at the heart of the vocation. The main criticism in terms of the social inclusion agenda is that the aims are highly idealistic, with little in the way of substance to assist in their implementation. The support mechanisms that are in place do not recognise that to achieve the goals that have been set involves the mobilisation of social change, as much of it is based within attitudinal and cultural contexts. In addition the distribution of resources to support the action plan was limited and inconsistent, with short-term project funding being offered rather than long-term coherent provision.

Figure 2.3 provides an overview of the social inclusion agenda and the various strategies that are in place to support the stated aims. It also considers the possible barriers to fruition from social perspective.

The two highlighted goals sections within Figure 2.3 – employment and making it happen – are not aligned directly with the NSF. However, they do appear elsewhere in the policy framework.

Figure 2.3: Strategies and barriers to social inclusion

Aims	Strategies	Barriers
Stigma and discrimination (NSF Std 1)	<ul><li>Mental health promotion across provisions</li><li>Service accessibility</li><li>Positive media campaigns</li><li>Educational material</li><li>'Myth' busting</li><li>User organisations</li></ul>	<ul><li>Social norms</li><li>Public opinion</li><li>Political climate</li><li>Media portrayal</li><li>Identity/roles</li><li>Stereotyping</li><li>Historical beliefs</li></ul>
Role of health and social care (NSF Std 4)	<ul><li>Expert by experience</li><li>User organisations</li><li>Representation/involvement</li><li>CSCI and NICE standards</li><li>Education and advocacy</li><li>Evidence-based services subject to scrutiny</li></ul>	<ul><li>Resources and capability</li><li>Services are stigmatising</li><li>Professional role identity</li><li>Historical user experience</li><li>Time to build evidence base</li><li>Tokenistic involvement strategies</li></ul>
Employment	<ul><li>Supported employment schemes</li><li>Disability Discrimination Act</li><li>Equality Act 2006</li><li>Employment law</li><li>Supported vocational training and advisory services</li></ul>	<ul><li>Engagement of employers</li><li>Stigma and stereotyping</li><li>Resources to support</li><li>Capitalism and competition</li><li>Lack of additional employee support outside health and social care sector</li></ul>
Supporting families and community participation (NSF Std 6)	<ul><li>Community based services</li><li>Drop-in and direct access</li><li>Emphasis on psychosocial intervention including family work</li><li>Supported access to mainstream services</li><li>Occupational/vocational care planning</li><li>Direct payments and individual budgets</li></ul>	<ul><li>Breakdown of traditional community</li><li>Stigma and stereotyping</li><li>Choice versus protection</li><li>Public perception of risk</li><li>Defining 'reintegration'</li><li>Closure of rehabilitation services</li><li>Resources and difficulty accessing funding</li></ul>
The basics (NSF Std 3)	<ul><li>Supported accommodation</li><li>Floating support schemes</li><li>Rent deposit schemes</li><li>Specialist housing support</li><li>Money and debt management</li></ul>	<ul><li>Shortage of affordable housing</li><li>Engagement of providers</li><li>Market competition</li><li>Modern lifestyles</li></ul>
Making it happen	<ul><li>CSCI regulation standards</li><li>Local implementation plans</li><li>CSIP and SET support</li><li>Policy framework promoting inclusion agenda</li></ul>	<ul><li>Fragmented legal framework</li><li>L/T resource investment</li><li>Based on view of society</li><li>Measurability</li><li>One of many priorities</li></ul>

In the case of employment, this is a core standard within the CSCI regulation schedule, which states that all services providing social care must demonstrate a commitment and strategy to support the aim that all service users should be able to make a positive contribution within their communities. This standard includes such aspects as employment, as this is an activity that assists the individual to maintain an identity and sense of purpose within society.

In the case of 'making it happen', social inclusion is a key feature within both the modernisation agenda and the evidence base for effective service provision, and is enshrined within a range of legislation. While the implementation plan for the social inclusion agenda is fragmented across several policies, it remains a key focus for service providers and society as a whole.

Figure 2.3 demonstrates that there is a range of both strategies and barriers to the achievement of social inclusion. This is not intended as a definitive list and many initiatives are being delivered on both a national and local level to promote the agenda further. The aim here is to demonstrate that while the policy direction is being developed and supported there remain a number of obstacles, many of which relate to community engagement and attitudinal issues. These are obstacles that may potentially take a generation to resolve and the social work profession is needed to support the initiatives and promote the core values of challenging and questioning: 'Rome was not built in a day', as the saying goes.

Social work as a profession, and social care as a perspective, have been striving for many years to promote inclusion for those considered the most vulnerable in society, and have a key role to play in the social inclusion agenda.

The concept of stigma: how can social change be mobilised?

The perceptions of mental health and mental illness are societal constructs (Tew, 2005a), and many stereotypes and prejudices exist within the UK. These are driven by a range of factors, from media portrayal to presumption and negative experience. For many members of the public the experience of mental illness is attached to such derogatory terms as 'psycho' and 'nutter' and associated with images of violence and suicidal behaviour. Understanding of these behaviours and the recognition that the cases that are reported in the media are the exception, not the rule, is limited. This is not intended as a criticism of the British public – why and how should individuals be aware of these factors unless they have had direct experience of them?

Knowledge of the subject is often via political and media presentation and is subject to both bias and spin. In many cases direct experience is disconnected from the wider view. The phenomenon of identifying one person with a mental health label as no threat because they are a friend or family member, and as such not part of the 'potential danger' category, is widespread (Kessler et al., 1999; Byrne, 2000). This selective prejudice is difficult to address as the disconnection of beliefs for certain individuals does not allow for learning from experience. While this is not the case with all members of society, it is certainly a recognised state that is difficult to address in terms of education and the reduction of stigmatising attitudes and beliefs.

The impact of labelling

The label that an individual has also presents a range of negative connotations; for example, someone diagnosed as schizophrenic is considered far more dangerous than someone diagnosed as depressive or anxious (Martin et al., 2000; Lauber et al., 2006). This diversity in levels of prejudice suggests a complex societal system that will involve widespread attention in order to disentangle it. The very act of seeking help for a mental health difficulty can have stigmatising consequences for the individual, as the wider social network will have preconceived ideals of what being a mental health patient means. As a result of these preconceived ideas any person within this category can potentially face disadvantage. In addition, widespread research has been carried out in terms of professional groups and stigmatisation, and the findings suggest that the very people who are offering care and support are often the most prejudiced (Lauber et al., 2006; Read and Law, 1999). Issues such as risk aversion and overemphasis on protection are key factors in contributing to an individual's experience of discrimination and stigma.

The UK is on the whole viewed as a tolerant and liberal society, with anti-discriminatory legislation and values; however, the mental health population still experiences significant discrimination, often in passive forms. From a lower likelihood of securing and maintaining adequate housing, to being more likely to be long-term unemployed, these issues can often be directly attributed to passive prejudice. While our legislation states that equality of opportunity should be central to all processes, there remains a higher likelihood that an individual with a mental health problem will experience poverty and isolation and be dependent upon social welfare in its various forms (Thornicroft, 2006).

With these issues still prevalent with society, it is not too much of a leap to suggest that while the principles of the social inclusion agenda are based on principles that the majority support, the process of applying these principles is not an easy task. Attention will need to be paid to the whole range of indirect discrimination and prejudice that users of mental health services experience in the various aspects of their lives, and interactions with wider society.

Despite this discussion, the direction of the social inclusion developments remains consistent with both social care values and improving the service user experience. It is necessary that these aims are in place; however, it is also necessary that a realistic timeframe and strategy are also developed to deliver what is undoubtedly an essential piece of the policy and service direction.

The well-being agenda

Continuing the theme of inclusion and empowerment, the 2005 green paper *Independence, Well-being and Choice* and the subsequent 2006 white paper – *Our Health, Our Care, Our Say* set out the vision for integrated health and social care services that placed service users in the driving seat of care provision. The key themes of the white paper were:

- helping people to lead healthier and more independent lives

- the need to provide more responsive and accessible care

- better support for people with ongoing needs

- a wider range of services in the community

- ensuring that the reforms put people in control. (DoH, 2006)

As with the modernisation and social inclusion agendas, the themes of the white paper are consistent with the NSF standards and also marked the first major policy development that was explicit in the support of integrated services. This document was the first joint white paper to be issued and thus a landmark piece of the framework within which services operate. Again, the focus on social care principles is evident, and the social work profession is secure within its knowledge and value base. There is a definite move towards self-determination within policy and widespread emphasis is placed upon improving the service user experience.

One key consideration within the well-being agenda, and in fact the social inclusion agenda, is that the definition of what it means to the individual is very subjective. Issues such as experience, belief systems and personal expectations all contribute to what a person views as part of or essential to well-being. This lack of universal definition is potentially a positive attribute, as it can enable the service users to define their own goals and express their individual aspirations. The danger in this case, however, is that professionals may place their own interpretation of well-being upon the service user, and this does not empower but potentially creates a dependency or resistance towards engagement with the service. The professionals' tendency to take the lead and place themselves as 'expert' (which can, and does, include the social work profession), is a definite risk. Workers in the field need to keep in mind the core value of 'identifying and addressing their own prejudices and the potential impact on service users' as a critical factor within interactions and general practice to mitigate any potential influence. The service user is the expert when it comes to defining what well-being means to him or her.

Many service user groups have been established over the last decade, and are assisting in the process of informing and shaping services, although it is also the case that front line services are struggling to create a fully inclusive and involved consumer population. The criticism remains that professionals are not adept at handing control over to service users; external factors such as risk and stigmatisation make this especially the case within mental health services.

Social care outcomes and the inspection framework

The new CSCI inspection standards, against which services are assessed, were also derived from the green paper (supported by the white paper). These are a clear attempt to shift provision emphasis away from outputs and process, and towards outcomes that are meaningful for service users.

The measurement of these standards are still process-driven; however, the umbrella standards are a distinct development in terms of creating service user-focused and goal-orientated services. These standards are as follows:

1. improved health and emotional well-being

2. improved quality of life

3. protection from discrimination and harassment

4. economic well being

5. personal dignity

6. making a positive contribution

7. choice and control

8. leadership

9. commissioning and use of resources. (CSCI, 2007a)

Standards 8 and 9 are focused upon the actual provision of services – how these are administered and how the social care perspective is led and promoted within multi-disciplinary environments. The other seven standards relate directly to the potential impact that services need to be achieving for and with the users of services.

Currently the health and social care regulation regimes are not consistent with the wider policy framework of integrated provision, as discussed in Chapter 1. The next major development will be the merging of CSCI and health care inspection agencies, along with the Mental Health Act Commission. This is scheduled to become fully operational by 2009. At present there are separate regulation regimes, each with a slightly different emphasis.

The health care inspection service, known as the Health Care Commission (HCC), has as its framework, known as standards for better health (also termed core standards), a range of indicators relating to how services are delivered. The intention is that these will be combined with the CSCI standards, noted above, to create a comprehensive health and social care inspection system against which all agencies can be measured. This process will unify and align the provision of health and social care services with the wider legislative and policy contexts and ensure that providers are delivering evidence-based and effective interventions across the system.

Pieces of a jigsaw: fitting them all together

This chapter has attempted to outline the key agendas involved in the development of mental health care across the UK. Different areas have implemented the frameworks in slightly different ways, and discrepancies remain in the types and criteria for accessing services depending on the locality.

There is a requirement to provide a basic level of certain services, and all those who may require support from mental health professionals should therefore now be able to access it based on their assessed need at any given point. The tiers of service and engagement between primary and specialist care which are promoted within the NSF mean that any individual may approach his or her GP and be guaranteed to receive some type of service to meet the presenting needs appropriately. Although standardisation is still some time away, it is hoped that initiatives such as the combination of health and social care services, policies and regulation will aid this process and halt the discriminatory nature of the so called 'postcode lottery' (Dix, 2004; Sage, 2006; Ross, 2007).

Throughout this discussion an attempt has been made to relate each agenda and framework to the previous ones; Figure 2.4 provides a visual representation of this linkage.

As illustrated here, each initiative is connected to the others with the aim of creating a whole-systems approach that places the service user and the goal of recovery as central to the process. The frameworks combine process, provision and outcomes in attempt to create a map of how and why services operate.

The key element within social care is always the service user, and the relationship of that service user to his or her psychological and social world. This includes the relationship between the service user and the social worker as a key aspect of provision. The agendas operating within mental health service development are highly complementary to the perspective, and it appears that at this time, more than previously, the social care perspective is receiving support and attention.

The concept of recovery is still in development within services, and will be discussed in detail in Chapter 4. Despite this, it appears that the policy direction for mental health services on a strategic and operation level is attempting to make a difference to people's lives rather than to maintain the individual's illness, which is a criticism that has historically been directed at the discipline of psychiatric care (Frese et al., 2001; Ralph et al., 2002; Anthony, 1993).

Figure 2.4: Interaction of policy frameworks

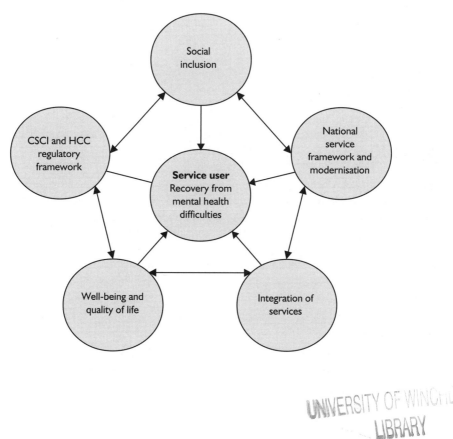

The policy direction and framework

Hubert Humphrey, quoted at the beginning of this chapter, stated that the moral test of government was how it treated the most vulnerable. While the current system is by no means free from criticism, the overall ethos and underlying principles are service user-focused and aimed at improving the overall well-being and inclusion of those who need services. At all times within the policy direction, the service user experience is key to all developments and provisions. The principle of a needs-led rather than service-led strategy, within a framework of evidence-based and inclusive practice, is a significant development and while there is still some way to go to achieve these ideals, professionals within the field agree that the principles are worth supporting.

Given that approximately one in six of the population will have some form of mental distress at any one time, this is an encouraging picture for us all. It is particularly complementary for social work practice as it maintains the core values and principles that are central to the profession.

Further reading

Department of Health (2006) *Our Health, Our Care, Our Say*. London: TSO.

Social Exclusion Unit (2004) *Social Exclusion and Mental Health: Social Exclusion Unit Report*. London: ODPM.

Chapter 3

The social work identity within mental health services

An identity would seem to be arrived at by the way in which the person faces and uses his experience. (James Baldwin, 1929–1987, US author)

PQ framework

Achieving Post-qualifying Social Work awards

This chapter will assist in the meeting of National Occupational Standards for Social Work:

Key Role 6, Unit 19:   Work within agreed standards of social work practice and ensure own professional development.

Key Role 6, Unit 21:   Contribute to the promotion of best social work practice.

For registered social workers considering, or working towards, post-qualifying awards this chapter will also assist in meeting the requirements of both the specialist award in mental health, and the national occupational standards in mental health which are core to the post-qualification standards in this area.

MHNOS 57:   Monitor, evaluate and improve processes for delivering mental health services to a population.

MHNOS 67:   Encourage stakeholders to see the value of improving environments and practices to promote mental health.

PQ Specialist Award in Mental Health:

47 (ii)   Applying knowledge, understanding and skill in relevant legal and policy frameworks.

47 (vii)   Promoting the social model of need/disability/mental health within multi-disciplinary settings.

Introduction

The nature of the roles and tasks of social work, and the professional contribution to multi-disciplinary working, are currently highly debated area (GSCC, 2007a; NIMHE, 2006). This chapter does not seek to add to the overall debate, but rather to explore the issue within the context of modern mental health services.

If social work is to function competently within an 'integrated' service framework, it is imperative that professionals are able to articulate and identify their contributions and perspectives (Bogg, 2007; Payne, 2006; Higham, 2006). The days of stating an opinion as a professional judgement, without explaining the evidence, are now quite rightly behind us and in order to retain credibility social workers are required to use and demonstrate evidence-based approaches in their work.

With this in mind the aims of this chapter are twofold: first, to develop an understanding of what professionalism in mental health social work means, and second, to highlight this understanding within the current service development framework.

The concept of social work professional identity

Identity is both a social and a psychological construct; it is the understanding that each individual develops in order to understand his place in the world. In theoretical terms the concept of social identity theory was defined by Tajfel and Turner (2001) who highlighted two key factors as part of the human conditions:

- that individuals strive for a positive self-image
- that this self-image is based upon both personal and social identities according to the groups whose values and beliefs best match their own.

Professional identity is part of this identification, and relies on the individual developing identification with the values and beliefs of a particular professional group. Individuals develop a notion of their chosen profession and form a personal alliance between their personal values and that of the group as they understand it to be.

Professional identity in mental health social work

The mental health social worker needs to have an overall understanding of a range of areas in order to develop a strong sense of identity and identification as a professional. The overview of all the areas is the basis of professional confidence, and hence the ability to function and fully contribute to a multi-disciplinary service environment. This understanding is based upon a number of elements, as illustrated in Figure 3.1.

The details of these aspects are outlined below: this list is not exhaustive, but rather aims to demonstrate the core elements of a mental health social worker and therefore the areas that an individual will relate to in order to develop a sense of professional identity within this field. It is suggested that concepts of all six areas are required for a social worker to have a solid and articulated professional identity.

Figure 3.1: Aspects of professional identity

(Developed from Tajfel and Turner, 2001; McGowen and Hart, 1990; Carpenter and Platt, 1997; Niemi, 1997)

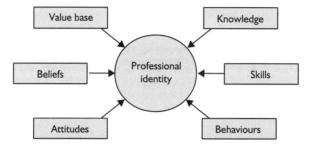

- *Knowledge*

  Roles, responsibilities and expectations, including statutory duties. In the case of mental health this will constitute a thorough understanding of mental health and community care legislation as well as policy and guidance such as the Care Programme Approach (CPA) and the National Service Framework (NSF).

- *Skills*

  Counselling, advocacy, assessment and care planning, including the use of structured psychosocial interventions, and the ability to respond to crisis by mobilising social and service networks.

- *Values*

  Person-centred, but with the ability to balance the core values of care and control. Protection is as much of a right as a liberty, and as a mental health social work professional the worker will be required to walk the line between the two in the best interests of service users.

- *Beliefs*

  A belief in, and commitment to, the recovery model and an emphasis on the core social care outcomes of independence, improved health and well-being for the individual. These core beliefs will once again need to be balanced with the belief that actions are taken in the best interest of the service user as there are occasions when actions are taken against individuals' wishes in order to protect them from harm.

- *Attitudes*

  Recovery is possible, and the worker is required to suspend his or her own beliefs and values to ensure that the individual's strengths, needs and aspirations are accounted for at all times. Persistence and patience are key attitudes to develop.

- *Behaviours*

  Anti-discriminatory and anti-oppressive practice, taking whatever action is necessary within professional boundaries to build relationships and respond to service user needs.

With these elements (or variations upon the themes, as each individual experiences the world slightly differently) in place, the social worker has the basis for a sound development of professional identity. These aspects of the identity have evolved and developed over the years; the value base is the only element which is static. Social work is built upon a value base that recognises the rights of the individual and places ethical practice as central to the profession (CCETSW, 1995; Young and Ashton, 1956; Banks, 1998). The other aspects, however, are subject to change and the role of the social worker is dependent on the social, political and economic environment in which it operates (Muijen, 2003; Lymbery, 2001; Payne, 2006); the historical context of the profession is therefore relevant to provide context for future discussion.

Reflection point

What elements are important within your understanding of your professional identity?

The historical context of mental health social work

Social work identity, or at least the beginnings of its development, can be traced back in mental health terms to the first psychiatric social workers who were operating in the UK during the 1920s (DoH, 2007a). This group used psychosocial methods to explain and approach mental distress. Over the next 20 years this group began to develop a distinct value base on which they based their practice. The social work contribution was recognised in these early years by the British Medical Association (BMA) who in 1939 offered to register social workers as medical auxiliaries. The offer was refused. The benefits of a registered, and therefore accountable, workforce was not in debate; however, social workers by this time had developed a strong commitment to social justice and welfare and it was felt that the BMA was not able to meet their needs or identify with their developing value base (DoH, 2007a). This stance marked the first clear challenge by the social work profession towards autonomy and independence, two dimensions that are now integral to the practice of mental health social workers (Lymbery, 2001; Gilbert, 2003; Smith, 2001; Evans et al., 2005).

Following the enactment of the 1946 NHS Act, local authorities became the main providers of social care services; the agencies responsible 'sprang directly from the poor laws' (Jordan, 1979). This allowed for the development of agencies whose principles were in line with the newly incepted welfare state, and the social work workforce began their migration from health, and charitable and privately run organisations (such as the Victorian asylums), into employment with local authority welfare-based organisations (Langham, 1993; Cree, 2002; Gilbert, 2003).

Mental health law and its impact on social work practice

The ratification of the 1959 Mental Health Act marked the next stage of professional development for social work. The role of the mental welfare officer (MWO) was accepted by the profession, and as a result it provided a statutory and legislative legitimisation that had not previously been in evidence. A significant element of the task of the MWO was to provide a counter-balance to medical opinion, and social workers, with their social justice value base, were ideally placed to undertake this task. It can be argued that the shift in emphasis in psychiatric provision was more to do with resources and the increasing costs of a long-term hospital population rather than a genuine commitment to welfare; but whatever the basic cause, social workers were moving from being a largely charitable enterprise into a legitimate and statutory role within mental health service provision. These changes were occurring within the context of an increased optimism towards the effectiveness of treatments and the development of more community-based approaches (Gilbert, 2003), and it appeared that the social work profession was beginning to find its niche.

The Mental Health Act 1983 continued the progression towards professionalism for social work by creating the Approved Social Work (ASW) role. The value base, which had been implicit in the 1959 Act and throughout the history of the profession, was now in statute. This created an ability in the ASW workforce to articulate and represent their views and contribution to service provision in a coherent and supported way, and shifted the balance of power away from the medical profession (Gilbert, 2003; Walton, 2000; Sheppard, 1990). Section 13 of the Mental Health Act sets out the ASW role and clearly states that any application for compulsion is the responsibility of the social worker; the medical role is one of diagnosis and treatment, but not to make the decision to detain (Jones, 2006). This was a significant step forward for the profession and for the definition of the social work contribution to mental health service provision.

Approved Mental Health Professionals

The Mental Health Act 2007, which received royal assent in July 2007 and will be fully implemented in October 2008, is due to make amendments to the 1983 Act. This is a significant development for the social work profession; in particular, the role of the ASW is set to be extended to other professionals and will be known as the Approved Mental Health Professional (AMHP).

In addition, a new role of Responsible Clinician (RC) is being created, equivalent to the current Responsible Medical Officer (RMO), but without the medical practitioner requirement. Social workers will be free to train for the RC role and it is expected that the current ASW workforce will lead the transition to the AMHP.

The framework for the AMHP is based upon the social work values and ASW competency requirements, and the role remains one of independence and autonomy, and is required both to act in the best interests of the service user and to provide a counter-balance to the medical perspective. This is achieved by taking into account the social, psychological and economic factors associated with the individual's level of mental distress as part of the decision making process. Other professionals will be required to immerse themselves in a system that the social work profession has developed throughout its history. With these changes the social work contribution will again change, and there is the potential for the profession to play a significant role in the implementation of the new legislative processes.

Current trends

As already discussed in Chapters 1 and 2, the combined management of health and social care began with the enactment of the Health Act 1999; before this point agencies and professionals had worked together but within separate organisations with very separate remits. The NSF for Mental Health was also published in 1999, and again the focus was placed upon integrated services designed to promote mental health, reduce stigma and increase social inclusion of the service user group. The policy focus was shifting towards a more user-centric provision, recognising that mental health issues were a national concern, and constituted far more than just a medical problem. As a result of these policy shifts work commenced by a range of bodies to describe and define the role of workers within mental health services. As a result documents such as *The Capable Practitioner* (Sainsbury Centre for Medical Health, 2001) and *Ten Essential Shared Capabilities* (DoH, 2004) were published in attempt to define the skills and values that would be required to work within the new system.

Social work and mental health competency framework

The framework is not new to the social work profession: the concepts of competency-based training and working were introduced to social work in 1989, when the Diploma in Social Work was established. The then regulatory body – the Central Council for Education and Training in Social Work (CCETSW) – outlined a framework of six core competencies which all social workers had to demonstrate and evidence their practice against. These competencies were as follows:

- communicate and engage
- promote and enable
- assess and plan
- intervene and provide services
- working in organisations
- professional development.

(CCETSW, 1989, revised 1995)

A six-point value base was also part of the framework, and social workers were required to demonstrate an underpinning of this value base throughout all the core competencies. These related to anti-discriminatory practice principles (Thompson, 2001), and the values that had been within social work (i.e. social justice and human rights) since its earliest inception.

The CCETSW framework has now been superseded by the National Occupational Standards for Social Work (TOPSS, 2002) and the GSCC Code of Conduct (GSCC, 2002); however, the basic competency areas and value principles remain unchanged, and comparisons can there-fore be made. The capable practitioner appears to be a hybrid of these competencies. As Figure 3.2 demonstrates, each element in the Capable Practitioner has an equivalent competency from the original CCETSW framework.

Figure 3.2: The capable practitioner framework as it relates to social work

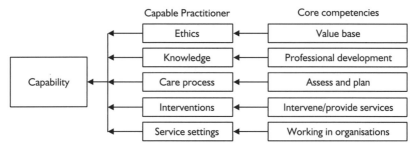

This framework represented a positive step for the social work profession within mental health, which was already familiar with the premises that capability was to be assessed against, and were thus at a distinct advantage in the process. Whereas health colleagues operated within a medical model framework that concentrated on diagnosis, containment and medical treatment of mental distress (Bentall, 2004; Read et al., 2004) the social model takes a whole-systems approach, considering social, psychological and economic factors as inter-dependent elements in the creation and maintenance of an individual's distress (Tew, 2005a; Golightly, 2006). The capable practitioner framework recognised the social model and indicated a range of skills, knowledge and values that a practitioner would need in order to promote the best interests and individual care needs of the service user group.

The next stage of the workforce development plan, *The Ten Essential Shared Capabilities* (DoH, 2004), aimed to develop the original framework set out by *The Capable Practitioner* and identify key areas that all workers, regardless of professional background, were required to develop in order to deliver socially inclusive and recovery-orientated services. Once again the social work values and skills were evident, and although there was no explicit statement that this was the case there are clear similarities that can be drawn. Figure 3.3 demonstrates these common elements in terms of the National Occupation Standards, the GSCC Code of Practice, and also the original Code of Ethics that was set out by the British Association of Social Workers. It is clear from this illustration that Social Work as a profession was in a strong starting position within the modern mental health service provision.

The fact that mental health practice requirements within the modern services are similar to those which historically been the premise of social work would suggest that of all the professions, social workers would find it easiest to adapt and lead on the agenda. This has been highlighted by commentators on the issue, as Carpenter suggested in 2002:

> *Social Workers are well suited to the tasks of answering the mandate of the recovery paradigm . . . social work could once again define its distinct professional role while simultaneously engaging with consumers to redefine the mental health system.*
> (Carpenter, 2002, p. 92)

With this being the case, it appeared that while the ADSS and the GSCC expressed their support for the capability framework and policy direction in the form of a discussion paper examining the social work role (NIMHE, 2006), social workers on the whole were remarkably reserved in their responses.

Figure 3.3: A comparison of the professional frameworks

Ten Essential Shared Capabilities, 2004	National occupational standards, 2002 (Appendix 2)	GSCC Code of Practice, 2002 (Appendix 3)	BASW Code of Ethics, 1977 (Appendix 1)
Partnership	Key role 3	1.2, 3.1, 3.7, 4.1	Core principle 4
Diversity	Key role 1,2, 3	1.1, 1.6	Core principle 1
Ethics	Principles	2.1–2.7, 3.5, 3.8, 5.1–5.8	Core principle 1, 4
Challenge inequality	Key role 4	1.5, 3.1, 3.8, 5.1–5.8	Core principle 1, 2
Recovery	Key role 2	1.1, 1.3	Core principle 1, 2
Needs and strengths	Key role 3	1.1, 1.3, 3.1	Core principle 1, 2
Service user-centred care	Key role 2, 3	All	Core principle 1, 2, 3
Make a difference	Key role 3, 4	3.4, 3.7	Core principle 3
Safety and positive risk	Key role 4	3.2, 3.3, 3.7, 4.1–4.1, 5.1–5.8	Core principle 5
Professional development	Key role 5,6	5.1–5.8, 6.1–6.8	Core principle 5

Reflection point

What are your experiences of capability frameworks and how do these relate to your understanding of social work professional identity?

Social Work National Occupational Standards

The introduction of the National Occupational Standards was a landmark step for social work in that it enshrined the notion of professionalism that had been long awaited for many. At the same time the formation of the General Social Care Council (GSCC) and the registration of social workers was introduced. Statute dictated that the title of 'social worker' was now protected and it became a criminal offence to use the title without qualification and registration. Despite these steps, the Occupational Standards came into being with little fanfare and there was scant evidence that the steps strengthened the profession. For a profession that had been striving for recognition of its particular contribution the lack of comment raised many questions in regard to whether an 'identity crisis' was occurring (NIMHE, 2006; Powell, 2001; Payne, 2007).

The British Association of Social Work (BASW) has at present a membership of approximately 11,000; according to the GSCC there are 78,000 registered social workers in the UK. In addition to these two bodies there is also a range of other organisations such as CSCI, Skills for Care, and the Department of Health who commentate, regulate and set targets and standards for social work and social care services. Whereas the medical and nursing professions both have Royal Colleges to represent their professional needs and views, social workers have no such equivalent to identify with.

Question

Could the lack of identification with a central body, which speaks for professionalism and identity, serve partly to explain the apathy of the profession?

Inter-professional practice: implications for social work identity

In order for a team to be effective there is a requirement for a sense of cooperation and common purpose. There is extensive evidence concerning effectiveness of team working, but for the purposes of this text the work carried out by Anderson and West (1998), who outlined an inventory to test the level of functioning of a team, will be considered. While other studies also have value in this discussion, this model highlights many of the common factors and places them within a framework that will be readily understood and utilised by both health and social care professionals. It is consistent with the professional needs of the workers involved, and also provides a correlation to both the continuing professional development and service improvement concepts within modern mental health services.

Each of these areas is important when considering team identification: the professionals involved need to identify with and own the team's purpose and goals if there is to be effective multi-disciplinary cooperation. The social work profession has a history of independence and autonomy, but there is also a strong culture of participation and supportive supervisory relationships (Brown and Bourne, 1995; Kadushin, 1992). The impact of such a model on the professional identity is thus optimistic. There appears to be a plethora of anecdotal evidence from social workers suggesting that if the team environment is collaborative they are more likely to engage in the process of integration of services. However, when presented with hierarchical and top-down management, which is autocratic and bureaucratic, the result is fragmentation, conflict and a lack of engagement in the team process.

The structure and functioning of the NHS has long been one of directive management and medical dominance, which is in direct conflict with the culture in which social work operates, as the latter is based on values of self-determination, positive risk-taking and collaboration. While many practitioners are able to conceptualise and place an intellectual understanding upon the environment in which they work, the ability to practise within that environment is often restricted, which results in a lack of faith and morale among the workforce.

Figure 3.4: Team functioning inventory

---

1. Participation in team activity
To what extent do workers take part in decision-making and joint activities?
(For example team meetings, case reviews, planning meetings, recruitment of staff, and use of budgets)

2. Support for new ideas
Are staff optimistic and supportive of change within the team?
Do they feel able to utilise creative problem solving approaches?

3. Clarity of objectives
Is there a clear mission statement for the team?
Are workers signed up to joint objectives concerning what the team is attempting to achieve as its core business?

4. Task style
Is there clarity regarding what interventions are carried out and when these are employed?
Are the performance and governance frameworks in place and applied consistently across the professions working within the team?

5. Reviewing process
Is there a common review framework of team processes, regular team days in which all workers contribute and provide feedback regarding working dynamics?

6. Perceived organisational efficiency
To what extent is there a single management structure?
Are policies and procedures in place that are robust and supportive of evidence-based practice principles?
How is the organisation perceived by staff and is there a clear pathway for organisational processes that corresponds to the needs of the service?

7. Level of innovation
To what extent is creativity within the team supported?
Are staff autonomy and professional judgement respected and do staff feel able to use their skills and perspectives within their work?

(Adapted from Anderson and West, 1998)

Multi-disciplinary teams – what is the research evidence?

In terms of research evidence concerning the facets and effectiveness of multi-disciplinary team working the main sources are a number of small-scale studies that have been carried out with Community Mental Health Teams (CMHTs). These studies have a number of common themes, which contribute to difficulties in achieving integrated provision. These can be summarised as follows:

- *Role ambiguity and conflict*

  There is often a lack of clarity surrounding who does what and why within the multi-disciplinary team, and this is an area that often finds workers floundering. The lack of clarity and understanding between professionals means that for many the key element of professional respect, which according to Anderson and West (1998) is an essential element of team functioning, is lacking; workers therefore have a lack of identification with their colleagues and do not receive the level of support and collaboration that should be an integral part of multi-disciplinary functioning.

- *Communication difficulties*

  The differing perspectives and approaches among professionals have created cultural and language differences: as each of the parent organisations (NHS and social services departments) have grown up, so have the pathways and communication facets within them. The ability to speak the same language is something which is key to collaborative working practices, and there remains a key difference between the professions in terms of their conceptual frameworks, priorities and perspectives.

- *Development of a shared philosophy*

  The competing dominance of the medical and social models when considering mental distress is a clear stumbling block, and teams need to develop a shared approach and ethos in order to work effectively together. This does not mean that all professionals need to adopt the same approach – the generic elements of mental health workers are not ideals that this text supports – but rather an emphasis on the common goals need to be agreed, to ensure that while the path each profession takes may differ the destination remains the same for all. (This is an area that will be discussed in more detail in Chapter 4.)

- *Lack of faith in management understanding and effectiveness*

  There appears to be a lack of faith within professional groups in the management structures within service delivery. This is often a result of resentment to organisational and resource restrictions, which are perceived as having an adverse impact upon professional practice as they are often not adequately explained and as such are viewed as a control mechanism (Hafford-Letchfield, 2006). The role of the team manager is a relatively new discipline and is often seen by workers as an administrative task that places organisational needs above clinical needs. The professionals involved often are pessimistic in their belief that management structures are able to support the development of professional practice. This situation has a negative impact upon multi-disciplinary working, as all groups require leadership and it is often the case that the perceived leader of the team is failing to represent their professional interests; there is thus a tendency to return to self-reliance, which creates fragmentation within the team environment.

- *Power and hierarchy/Uni-professional cultures*

  The issue of prominence of any one profession creates an atmosphere of threat and insecurity. In the same way as individuals in any society react to threat with a 'fight or flight' reaction, so to do professional groups. The work of Peck and Norman (1999) highlighted this issue and explored the understanding each profession had of the others within the multi-disciplinary arena. The findings highlighted the tendency for groups either to isolate themselves or to take an aggressive stance in any potential collaborative effort when they felt they were either being marginalised or discounted; the value of each professions unique contribution to the care processes and service delivery therefore needs to be equitable.

- *Perspective and priority conflicts.*

The contribution in terms of priorities and perspectives of professionals within the multi-disciplinary team is often overlooked as organisations strive for equality. There is a misconception that equality means being the same and this is not the case. As already stated the path each professional group takes may differ, but the goal, in terms of quality service delivery and enhancing the service user experience, is common and the approaches that each group brings to the team are invaluable in terms of viewing the service user within his or her biopsychosocial contexts. The priority that a social worker brings will differ substantially from the priority of the medical staff and these differences need to be understood and embraced, as they provide the basis of a holistic treatment process.

(Weinstein et al., 2003)

(*See also* Peck and Norman, 1999; Norman and Peck, 1999; Fitzsimmons and White, 1997; Carpenter et al., 2003; Gibb et al., 2002; Anderson and West, 1998, for full details of the research evidence in this area.)

Social work identity and multi-disciplinary teams

The social work identity within the multi-disciplinary team is a contested issue. It is also the case that nursing, occupational therapy and medical staff groups are having the same types of debates, of which the document *Mental Health: New Ways of Working* (DoH, 2007a) is the end result within mental health. The integration of services has created discomfort across all the professional groups and social work is no exception. The implications of the expansion of the ASW role, and the debates around definition of the social work tasks, have created unease within the profession, and it has become necessary to make such definitions in order to achieve multi-professional understanding. It also needs to be recognised that the emphasis on what were previously seen as traditional social work values has left many social workers feeling excluded, and the perceived 'take-over' of the health service and the medically dominated structures has contributed to these feelings.

While many have noted that social workers are actually well-placed to take a lead on the integration and social inclusion agendas, few staff feel in a position to do so, as they have become overwhelmed by the organisational structures and environments of the NHS, as one social care leader commented when questioned by the author:

It is only through embedding staff throughout the system and taking an active role . . . that we can prevent the social care voice from being subsumed by the behemoth that is the NHS.

(Dr Nick Hervey, Head of Social Care. South London and Maudsley NHS Foundation Trust)

Reflection point

To what extent does your employment environment affect how you define your professional role and identity?

Conclusions: the social work identity within mental health services

This chapter opened with James Baldwin's assertion that identity is a combination of how the individual faces and uses his experience. A range of frameworks within current mental health policy have been presented, and these tend to support the social model. In this respect mental health social workers have a distinct advantage; however, it seems that the professional identity and contribution of the profession to service provision is in a constant state of flux. So how do workers articulate and present their 'distinct' perspective?

It is argued that professional identity is constructed from a number of aspects, and that these combined provide the foundation for approach. Social work is a complex combination of attitudes, cultures, experiences and values that have evolved over time and the profession has had difficulty in articulating its roles and tasks. The differences in approach across the client groups (for example the distinction between child and adult social work) have exacerbated this lack of clarity, and the socio-economic impact upon the role further complicates any true definition, as social work by its very nature is dynamic.

The profession has traditionally been rooted in social inclusion, self-determination and individual rights, but as other professions have taken up these areas, instead of leading the way social workers on the whole appear to have withdrawn from the debate. This has further eroded their professional identity and credibility within the multi-disciplinary arena. Several pieces of work have been carried out to address this erosion, with commentary and involvement from a range of organisations such as BASW, NIMHE, CSIP, ADSS and GSCC, and *New Ways of Working* places significant value upon the social work contribution to modern mental health services. Despite these commentaries, however, social workers themselves need to step forward and articulate what they can offer to both the team and service developments. The profession's identity, within the context of policy frameworks, is essential to the its capability to do this effectively. While multi-disciplinary working does create the need for a range of generic skills, individual professional approaches and perspectives provide the added value, allowing a range of options and choices for the users of the service.

There is a wide range of theoretical and evidence-based approaches to draw upon, and a range of skills and knowledge within the profession, which all rest upon the very value base which mental health services now promote. Social work is unique, in that it recognises and is able to balance the conflicting agendas of both care and control. This is what social workers can offer, and what we must not lose sight of when entering into collaborative working arrangements and initiatives. This balance places social work in an ideal position to contribute to the effective development and delivery of services; the holistic view of mental health issues and societal responses provides a grounding which is invaluable and which research suggests is the key to recovery from mental ill health. This, combined with the ability to mobilise and coordinate responses and effectively network with other providers, should strengthen professional identity.

While the organisational driver for services may be the NHS, the policy context and framework are based upon the social model, and this needs to be recognised and focused upon by the staff involved. Workers need to be enabled to articulate their perspectives and identities effectively, so that services can learn from the wealth of available experience and develop in a user-focused manner.

Further reading

Higham, P. (2006) *Social Work: Introduction to Professional Practice.* London: Sage.

Payne, M. (2007) *What is Professional Social Work?* Bristol: BASW/Policy Press.

Chapter 4

The social perspective versus the medical perspective: have we found a middle ground?

You have your way; I have my way. As for the right way, the correct way, and the only way – it does not exist. (Friedrich Nietzsche, 1844–1900)

PQ framework

Achieving Post-qualifying Social Work awards

This chapter will assist in the meeting of National Occupational Standards for Social Work:

Key Role 5, Unit 17:   Work within multi-disciplinary and multi-organisational teams, networks and systems.

Key Role 6, Unit 21:   Contribute to the promotion of evidence-based practice.

For registered social workers considering, or working towards post-qualifying awards, this chapter will also assist in meeting the requirements of both the specialist award in mental health, and the national occupational standards in mental health which are core to the post-qualification standards in this area.

MHNOS 14:   Identify potential mental health needs and related issues.
MHNOS 94:   Enable people to recover from mental illness/distress.

PQ Specialist Award in Mental Health:

47 (vii)   Promoting the social model of need/disability/mental health within multi-disciplinary settings.

47 (x)   Utilising appropriate knowledge and research from other disciplines . . . contributing to the generation and promotion of evidence based practice.

Introduction

A range of theoretical perspectives are used to explain the nature of mental illness and its treatment, and it can appear that different professions adopt different theories. The premise of good practice may not be disputed, but the definition of it is dependent upon the perspective, and it is therefore necessary to examine a range of theories and evidence in order to achieve a holistic view of what works.

The aim of this chapter is to provide a comparison of the social and medical models of mental illness and mental distress, and to explore the possible impact of the application of these upon users of mental health care services. The integration of health and social care services has placed a requirement upon professionals to work together in a more coherent and coordinated way, and the aim here is to define a middle ground between the two perspectives.

This is not a new concept, and extensive work has been carried out in an attempt to create an evidence base that is accessible to a range of disciplines, and from which shared goals and a shared vision can be developed. Social work is an eclectic profession, which draws its knowledge and experience from a range of perspectives; this discussion can therefore inform the practitioners' theoretical knowledge in order to promote good evidence-based practice within mental health care.

What is good practice?

The principles of good practice within the field of mental health can be categorised into three key areas that interact and inform the individual profession or practitioner:

- theoretical base
- evidence base
- policy framework.

Figure 4.1 illustrates this interaction as it contributes to practice. The policy framework is something that is common to each profession, however the theory and evidence base is variable, and the following discussion will attempt to explore these variables in light of the research, evidence and literature available on the subject.

Figure 4.1: Good practice model

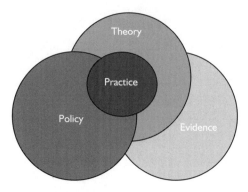

Identifying the theory base

In the field of mental illness there have traditionally been two key perspectives, the medical model and the social model. There has long been debate between the two, and there is a particular criticism among social model advocates that the medical model has been dominant and does not encompass the real range of influences and impacts upon mental ill health (Bentall, 2004; Double, 2002; Tew, 2002).

The anti-psychiatry movement of the 1960s and 1970s, which has now largely been discredited, and the subsequent critical psychiatry network, was one of the harshest critics of the medical model, and terms such as 'toxic psychiatry' and 'pseudo-science' have been in the literature since the writings of Laing (1960) and Szasz (1972). Despite these criticisms and comments the biomedical approach to mental illness has remained prevalent since the 1870s, when Emile Kraeplin first published his groundbreaking text *Compendium of Psychiatry*, the first edition of which was published in 1873 (Berrios and Hauser, 1988; Bentall, 2004). While developments have occurred, the basis of an illness-based diagnostic and classification system has remained at the core of medical-led psychiatric practice.

The social model of mental illness, in comparison, is a relatively new area, and while its origins can be dated back to the first psychiatric social workers (as discussed in Chapter 3), the modern approaches were not fully enshrined into common practice until the late 1970s, when community care approaches were adopted into governmental policy, and the 'survivor movement' began to be heard as a valid voice.

There are some key differences between the medical and social models, as Figure 4.2 illustrates.

Figure 4.2: The medical model and the social model of mental distress

Medical model	*Social model*
Disability is a fault, deficiency or abnormality in the individual	Disability is a difference
Being disabled is negative	Being disabled is neutral
Disability resides in the individual	Disability derives from interaction between the individual and society
The remedy for disability-related problems is cure or normalisation of the individual	The remedy for disability-related problems is a change in the interaction between the individual and society
The agent of remedy is the professional	The agent of remedy can be the individual, or anyone who affects the interaction between the individual and society
(Adapted from Gill, 1994)	

These two approaches are diametrically opposite, and each has a base of evidence and theory to draw upon.

The social model

The social model of disability rests on a key assumption, which is that it is the societal (and professional) response to the impairment that is the problem, not the impairment itself (Tew, 2002). This places the emphasis of the condition on the consequences of the mental distress or disorder, and is therefore one of the key areas that differ from the medical model. Instead of looking at symptoms and disorders as an entity in themselves, requiring treatment or cure, the social model focuses on the social consequences and how to improve the quality of life and wider responses to the difficulties the individual is facing. The diagnosis is not relevant in this perspective (Harris, 2000), but rather the implications, interactions with the environment and possible solutions to the difficulties. The social model argues that social factors such as isolation, socio-economic status, personal narrative, self-esteem and stress are the key factors in an individual developing a mental disorder (see Brown and Harris, 1978; Mirowsky and Ross, 1989; Wethington and Kessler, 1986; Williams, 1990; Pearlin, 1989; Bruce et al., 1991; Tew, 2005c).

There has been significant debate over recent years in regard to defining and developing a coherent evidence base for the social perspective. The Social Perspectives Network (SPN), a collaboration of service users, carers, professionals and agencies within the field, has published a number of papers in this vein, and has attempted to define the social model within modern mental health services. This definition is illustrated in Figure 4.3.

Figure 4.3: Defining the social model in mental health: key characteristics

It is based on an understanding of the complexity of human health and well-being.

It emphasises the interaction of social factors with those of biology and microbiology in the construction of health and disease.

It addresses the inner and outer worlds of individuals, groups and communities.

It embraces the experiences and supports the social networks of people who are vulnerable.

It understands and works collaboratively within the institutions of civil society to promote the interests of individuals and communities and to critique and challenge when these are detrimental to these interests.

It emphasises shared knowledge and shared territory with a range of disciplines, service users and the general public.

It emphasises empowerment and capacity building at individual and community level and therefore tolerates and celebrates difference.

It places equal value on the expertise of service users, carers and the general public but

> will challenge attitudes and practices that are oppressive, judgemental and destructive.
>
> It promotes a critical understanding of the nature of power and hierarchy in the creation of health inequalities and social exclusion.
>
> (Adapted from Duggan, 2002)

The social model places the service user at the centre of any process, and the expert on his or her own condition. While there is no debate that the service user is the focus, the medical model emphasises treatment and professional expertise rather than the service user leading the process, to the extent that the individual may not always be a consenting participant. While social work does to a certain extent appreciate this stance, with the role of the Approved Social Worker and legal detainment being the classic example, this is always within the context of the individual's rights and views and context, with an acute appreciation of the impact of power dynamics.

The medical approach can at times be seen as 'doing things to people' rather than 'doing things with them', and this is one of the key differences between the two models and the aspect that creates the most conflict in terms of reconciling and finding a middle ground from which the professions can seek a partnership approach.

Reflection point

What understanding and concepts of mental distress inform your practice?

The medical model

When the medical model is discussed in psychiatric terms, it is ordinarily a reference to the biological model. This rests upon two key principles: first, that mental disorder is a brain disorder, and second, that all mental events are neurological events (McLaren, 2007; Wade and Halligan, 2004; Double, 1990). This stance would presume that the social, cultural and environment issues, which are present in the individual's life, are a result of the mental condition rather than a part of it. Evidence does not, on the whole, support this stance in its purest form, but as medical training is heavily biased towards diagnosing and treating any given problem (Double, 2000), it is little surprise that psychiatry, as a branch of medicine, adopted this view.

The basic philosophy of the approach is that mental disorders, largely considered to be as a result of either chemical imbalance or other disease of the brain (Double, 1990; 2000), can be identified by the collection of presenting symptoms. These can then lead to a diagnosis and subsequent indication of treatment, usually chemotherapy (Fulford, 2005; Galatzer-Levy and Galatzer-Levy, 2007; Reiger, 2003). A plethora of clinical trials and research have been carried out since the widespread use of chlorpromazine (also known as Largactil) took hold in the 1950s, to provide the evidence base for pharmacology in psychiatric conditions (for examples of such work see Wahlbeck et al., 1999; Tuunainen et al., 2000; Bagnell et al., 2003; Geddes et al., 2000; Leucht et al., 2003).

The exact mechanisms of psychiatric drugs are often questioned and extensive (and changeable) research has been carried out to attempt to isolate genetic and biological causes of mental disorders. This has not yet been successful and there are many debates in the field as to whether such causes even exist; however, this does not change the fact that some medications can help some people. Key evidence of this has been demonstrated in the recent research into the use of antidepressant medication, carried out at the University of Hull. This work suggested that the use of such medication, while useful for some individuals, especially those with high degrees of depressive disorder, is not effective for others, with placebos being reported as having similar effects (Kirsh et al., 2008). This in itself gives some support to the need for diagnostic systems, whereby the practitioner needs to be able to identify the symptom clusters to be able to apply the treatment most likely to have effect.

The criticism of diagnostic categories (such as the stigma created by giving an individual a specific label) is not dispelled or underestimated by this discussion and a diagnosis can hold as much detriment as it can benefit; however, the classification systems in psychiatry (DSM 4 and ICD 10 – both of which are international classification systems used to assist the diagnosis of mental disorders based on presenting symptoms) have persisted due to the potential effectiveness of pharmacological treatments.

Though there are many and varied critics of the so-called medical model in psychiatry, there does appear to be significant evidence that pharmacological treatments can, and do, have an effect on the symptoms suffered by some patients. While this is not the whole story and is difficult to attribute to direct brain/body/genetic dysfunction, it can assist many individuals to better manage the symptoms from which they suffer, alongside the range of psychological and social interventions that have been developed.

This discussion does not seek to underestimate the influence or importance of social psychiatry or critical psychiatry, two branches that have significant emphasis on the interpersonal and cultural context of mental illness and well-being. Social psychiatry has been particularly associated with the creation of therapeutic communities since the early 1960s, the central philosophy of which is that service users are instrumental in their own, and other community members', recovery from mental distress (Kelly et al., 2004; Andreoli, 1997). These branches of psychiatry have undertaken significant work and research aimed at promoting a holistic theory and evidence base relating to treatment and recovery from mental illness.

> **Reflection point**
>
> What is the impact of a psychiatric diagnosis on your practice?

The biopsychosocial model

As a response to the rising criticisms of the medical model, the concept of combining the perspectives started to be discussed in the late 1970s. This was led by the work of Engel

(1977; 1980), who defined the origins of the biopsychosocial model. This was a significant piece of work, which stated that no one perspective was sufficient to understand and treat mental disorder and that the way forward was therefore to combine them all. The underpinning theory for the biopsychosocial model was the premise that biological, social and psychological factors all contribute to the cause and progression of a person's mental disorder and as a result each area needs to be treated (Engels, 1980; Kotsiubinskii, 2002; McLaren, 2007). Figure 4.4 provides an illustration of this approach and the potential treatments.

While the biopsychosocial model does take account of the range of impacts and influences upon mental disorder and distress, the emphasis remains upon the service user being treated by professionals. This does not fully account for individuals' experience or expertise in their own situation. As a result the model, while seen as the beginnings of a compromise, has been criticised for placing excessive emphasis on illness and treatment rather than relationships. This results in hierarchal and over-simplified links between three systems which are complex and difficult to identify (Richter, 1999; McLaren, 1998; 2007; Bartz, 1999).

The recovery model – finding the middle ground:

The definition of recovery is a contested area and it is dependent upon each individual's lived experience. The basic principle of the recovery model is that 'recovery is possible' in whatever form this takes for the person in question (Deegan, 1988; Anthony, 1993; Sullivan, 1997). The addiction field has long been concerned with this concept: in fact the 12-step model, originally developed for alcohol dependence in the 1930s by Bill Wilson and Dr Bob Smith (Wilson, 1957), centred upon the disease model of alcoholism and espoused the concept that while there may be no known cure, the progress of the disease can be arrested and then recovery is possible. The mental health field has, over recent years, embraced this understanding and the term 'recovery' is now often heard both within service delivery and academic contexts. The emphasis within mental health services upon psychosocial interventions is a key element within this model, with the concept of recovery being the core factor of the approach as it attempts to assist individuals to address the social and psychological issues within their lives.

Figure 4.4: The biopsychosocial model

	Symptoms	Treatment
Biological	Depression Psychosis Anxiety	Anti-depressants Anti-psychotics Sedatives
Social	Isolation Poverty Family breakdown	Social skills training Welfare Family therapy
Psychological	Lack of coping skills Low self-esteem Traumatic memory	Skills training Counselling Cognitive Behavioural Therapy (CBT)

One particularly useful definition of recovery was outlined in 2001 in California, by a Task Force set up by Contra Costra County which stated that recovery was:

> *both a conceptual framework for understanding mental illness and a system of care to provide supports and opportunities for personal development . . . while individuals may not be able to have full control over their symptoms, they can have full control over their lives . . . [patients] can achieve not only affective stability and social rehabilitation, but transcend limits imposed by both mental illness and social barriers to achieve their highest goals and aspirations.* (Mahler and Tavano, 2001)

Regardless of the definition of what recovery actually is, there are a number of principles upon which the literature on the subject appears to agree (Allott et al., 2002; Frese et al., 2001; Kelly and Gamble, 2005; Townsend and Glasser, 2003; Young and Ensing, 1999; Deegan, 1988; Anthony, 1993; Sullivan, 1997):

- it is a holistic view of mental illness that focuses on the person, not just the symptoms, and issues of human diversity need to be considered;

- it is not a function of any given theory about causes of mental illness;

- it is achievable and can occur even though symptoms may recur;

- individuals are responsible for the solution, not the problem;

- a well-organised support system is required to support recovery;

- consumer rights, advocacy, and social change are all important aspects of recovery.

These ideals are very similar in nature to the social model already discussed within this chapter, and it is thus no surprise that social care and social work practitioners have embraced the recovery model within mental health care. It appears that the medical practitioners within psychiatry have also accepted the concepts of the recovery model; with the Royal College of Psychiatry welcoming what is termed 'the common purpose' (RCP, 2007).

Reflection point

What does the term recovery mean to you?

Recovery and multi-disciplinary working

The inclusive nature of recovery has provided an opportunity for the disciplines to work in partnership, as it places equal value upon social, psychological and medical input. Each has something to contribute to the individual experience of mental health and mental illness. The individual is at the centre of any action and the emphasis is placed upon well-being and applying what works.

Sheila's case is an example of the success of the recovery model, with everyone working together towards a shared aim. It could be argued that hers is an ideal case and that many users of mental health services are not able to engage in this type of plan, or that the services

Figure 4.5: Case study example – Sheila

Sheila began to get ill when she was about 19 years old. She had some depression as a teenager but in her second year at university she started feeling that she was being followed and stopped going to classes. She started sleeping a lot, stopped eating and would not leave her flat. Her friends started to get worried and spoke to one of their lecturers about it who recommended that Sheila see the college counsellor.

Sheila spoke to the counsellor and told her how she was feeling, and she was referred to a psychiatrist at the university. Sheila saw the psychiatrist and told him all her symptoms. She says: 'I felt like people started looking like robots, my body seemed to be alien matter, I seemed to be like from outer space somehow.' The psychiatrist prescribed her some antidepressant and some anti-psychotic medication, but did not make a diagnosis at the time, saying he wanted to review how things went on.

This lasted about two years. Sheila was quite suicidal for that period, mainly because she did not know what was going on and was becoming more and more depressed. She had lost hope – she did not want anything to do with her family, friends or her studies, and she stopped contact with them all. She says 'I felt lost and alone, I had no idea what was happening to me or why.'

Sheila was admitted to hospital during this time, under section 2 of the Mental Health Act 1983. The medications were not working as she thought they would and she stopped taking them. After her admission Sheila was referred to a Community Mental Health Team and a psychiatrist; she also starting seeing a community psychiatric nurse (CPN) and a social worker, and was referred to a counselling psychologist and a day centre.

Recovery and the wellness plan

Sheila's community assessment took account of her symptoms, her social contact and isolation, activities, medication, and her psychological state.

Who did what?

Sheila:	Talked about how she felt and asked the questions she needed to
Psychiatrist:	Medication and symptom control
CPN:	Psychoeducation, health and monitoring of side effects
Social worker:	Family work, social networks, re-housing and relapse planning
Psychologist:	Short-term cognitive behavioural therapy to improve coping skills
Day centre:	Daily activities, support to re-enter education and complete studies
Her family:	Engaged in family work, listened to Sheila and learnt about her.

Sheila needed a range of input over a two-year period, which required several disciplines. She was able to access these and the various aspects of her life which she needed support with were addressed collaboratively with her. Her mental health problems are now in remission: she sees her GP regularly and is still prescribed antidepressants, and sees a counsellor via the primary care team once a month, which she calls her 'check-in'. Sheila has re-established contact with her family and they are all aware of her relapse plan should any re-emergence occur, including who to contact and what they each should do if they are concerned.

are unable to respond in such a way. This, however, does not negate the value of holistic care, or of service users' involvement in their own treatment. Each individual should be approached just as that, an individual, with individual needs and experiences; while diagnosis and medical treatment may be required (and in fact in some cases is essential), this is just part of the overall treatment plan, and all of the individual's needs should be accounted for to promote the best possible chances of recovery.

The whole-person approach is the central premise of the recovery model and also the linchpin of what makes it the potential middle ground between social and medical approaches. While medication and diagnosis are within the model, these are supported by collaboration, education and self-management and hence there is a general acceptance by both service users and professionals that this approach is a possible way forward and conducive to partnership and collaboration.

Social psychiatry has long since combined the social and medical perspectives, with a focus on the interpersonal. The discipline has applied a medical understanding and promoted interpersonal interactions as equal influences on the development and progression of mental disorder. The AESOP study carried out by the Institute of Psychiatry (Morgan et al., 2006) is a large scale, three-centre study that explored in detail the biological and social risk factors for psychosis and the interaction between the two. This study is a key example of social psychiatric research and one of many such research programmes.

The impact of the policy framework

Chapter 2 provided the framework for modern mental health services and demonstrated how concepts such as recovery, person-centred care and integrated multi-disciplinary approaches are central to policy that is aimed at creating modern, fit-for-purpose and socially inclusive models of service delivery. The conflict between the medical and social perspectives is not conducive towards meeting these aims, whereas the recovery model, as detailed, allows for the coming together of health and social services in a way that has not previously been possible.

In terms of this discussion, the direction of the policy framework encompasses the evidence base and theoretical groundings, so as to be relevant and applicable for the professions within it. The clinical guidelines published by NICE, HCC, SCIE and CSCI also take account of the recovery principles, and emphasise outcomes that are relevant to the users of services. This serves further to develop the theoretical and evidence base for mental health services. Due to the socio-economic nature of service delivery, it is difficult to develop a theoretical grounding that is contrary to the dominant political view, and while social work has overtly developed within the cultural and political arena (as discussed in Chapter 3), the impact upon the health professions has been more implicit. It can be suggested that psychiatry has always had more of a political slant than its general medical and physical cousins, and there are undoubtedly aspects of its history that can be ascribed to moral and social attitudes rather than any tangible scientific base. Regardless of whether the impact has been implicit or explicit, policy and politics have played their part. The integration of health and social care services and the broadening of professional roles and understandings within the framework have enabled the development of recovery-based provision, and have therefore had a direct impact upon professional practice, regardless of discipline.

The relationship between theory, evidence, and policy

As this discussion has demonstrated there is a clear linkage between theory, evidence and policy. The three areas operate on a continuum. The initial theory leads to a 'testing out' process, which produces the evidence, and in turn that evidence informs the policy direction and framework. No one area can operate in a vacuum and the practitioner needs to have a clear understanding of all three in order to apply best practice and professional development.

Social work has historically had a policy focus, and legislation has been on the curriculum since the first professional social work courses were developed. Mental health work is an area that has a particular emphasis in this context; this is as a result of factors such as public opinion and the devastation that can occur within society when mental health services are unable to meet the needs of the most complex individuals.

The whole-person approach needs to be mirrored in the professional 'tool-kit', regardless of discipline, and as such each element – whether it is theory, evidence, or policy – needs consideration within practice. Mental health service users are among the most vulnerable within our society, and they deserve to receive the best available care; this at times involves professionals putting aside their professional perspectives and prejudices and asking the question – what works for this person?

Have we found the common ground?

This discussion began with the premise that theory, evidence and policy were inter-related, and that all were required in order to develop and maintain good practice. The recovery model has been espoused as the way forward and it appears that perspectives that were diametrically opposed are finding agreement within this model. This text supports this model on a number of grounds, not least that it is wholly consistent with the values and principles of social work.

Policy is a dynamic entity, and it is recognised that there is a possibility that in the future, emphasis within service delivery may change. However, as long as there is a sound understanding of theory, and an awareness of emerging evidence regarding what works, the practice (for any profession) can and will remain grounded

As the initial words of this chapter from Nietzsche suggested, there is no one way that could be called the right way, and an individual's journey through mental health and illness is varied, so all professions have something to offer. There is no universal agreement on the correct approach; it is through debate, exploration and application that new approaches are developed.

The professional role is to support individuals (and at times their communities) through the experience, and to guide those affected, by ethical use of their understanding of the range of theory, evidence and policy available.

The coming together of health and social care provides an opportunity, as well a challenge.

The perspectives continue to have the potential to evolve and the common goal of improving people's quality of life remains the unifying factor: in the words of the 12-step fellowships, through emphasis on similarity rather than difference, recovery is possible.

Further reading:

Allott, P., Loganathan, L. and Fulford, K. W. M. (2002) Discovering hope for recovery. *Canadian Journal of Community Mental Health*, 21(2), 13–34.

Duggan, M. with Cooper, A. and Foster, J. (2002) *Modernising the Social Model in Mental Health: A Discussion Paper*. SPN Paper 1.

Chapter 5

Ownership and the secondment of social work staff

An employee's motivation is a direct result of the sum of interactions with his or her manager. (Dr Bob Nelson, author and motivational speaker)

PQ framework

Achieving Post-qualifying Social Work awards

This chapter will assist in the meeting of National Occupational Standards for Social Work:

Key Role 5, Unit 17: Work within multi-disciplinary and multi-organisational teams, networks and systems.

Key Role 6, Unit 21: Contribute to the promotion of best social work practice.

For registered social workers considering, or working towards, post-qualifying awards this chapter will also assist in meeting the requirements of both the specialist award in mental health, and the national occupational standards in mental health, which are core to the post-qualification standards in this area.

MHNOS 67: Encourage stakeholders to see the value of improving environments and practices to promote mental health.

MHNOS 79: Enable workers and agencies to work collaboratively.

PQ Specialist Award in Mental Health

47 (vii) Working collaboratively with other professions; promoting the social model of need/disability/mental health within multidisciplinary settings.

47 (xi) Influencing and supporting communities, organisations, agencies and services to promote people's mental health.

Introduction

One of the key integration models that have been adopted across mental health services, as part of the Health Act flexibilities, is that of secondment of staff into a multi-agency provision of services. The aim of this chapter is to explore the implications of this approach from the social care perspective, and address some of the issues that give rise to concern.

Management structures, accountability and governance are three issues that are central to this debate, alongside the potential effect that secondment can have both on the organisation and on the quality of services provided. Throughout this text a range of theoretical and practice-based approaches have been considered, and it is suggested that the mode of operation chosen by a particular organisation can have a direct impact upon the effectiveness of the partnership as a whole.

How secondment models are implemented can have a significant impact upon how they are received by those staff affected. It appears that in many instances, although there was a process of consultation, this was viewed as lip-service by many social care professionals. With this being the case, in many areas the integrative process was approached with a degree of negativity and suspicion by those involved, especially in the case of social work staff who viewed the secondment of their employment into the NHS as both a rejection from their original social services employers, and a 'take-over' by their health service hosts.

Social services departments, for their part, have had a tendency to second all services in their entirety, and the social work profession's links back to its social service roots have been significantly eroded by the process.

In addition to these consideration, issues such as the domination of the medical model, differences in statutory and legislative duties, and aspects of operation previously provided by social services, for example Mental Health Act assessments, being increasingly passed over to the NHS, have led to concerns as to whether professional identity and the independence of the social work role are sustainable within the health-dominated environment.

Whether these concerns are based on fear or fact has been debated elsewhere, but the fact that the anxiety exists is enough to constitute a risk to both employing organisations and the overall professional approach, and these areas therefore need to be addressed and considered within the overall integration agenda.

Organisational structure

In many areas, since the inception of the 1999 Health Act, the NHS has taken the role of lead agency for the provision of mental health services and the various partnerships that have been established.

The most common model of delivery is currently the co-location of health and social care professionals within community teams. This may be under one management structure or a number, dependent upon the area concerned. Figures 5.1 to 5.3 illustrate several of the common structures that have been adopted across the country. The aim here is to consider the costs and benefits of each of these structures, within the context of integrated care delivery.

Figure 5.1: Possible management structures 1

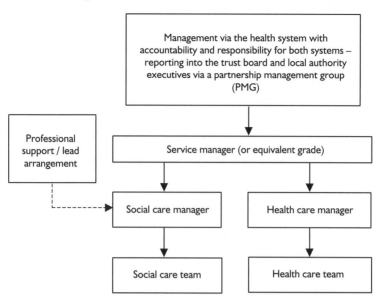

One of the key benefits of the model shown in Figure 5.1 is the duality of management and professionalism. Each discipline maintains a professional leadership structure, while an individual at service manager level is fully aware of the operational developments from both a health and social care service perspective.

The success of this approach is dependent upon strong leadership personnel and effective communication systems, two areas which are variable at the national level. In addition the majority of the service manager grade positions appear to have been filled by health personnel, many of whom do not have a sufficient understanding of social care perspectives, requirements or services in order to ensure that the discipline and strategic direction is fully represented.

As one social care leader operating within an NHS organisation stated:

> It is only through embedding staff throughout the system and taking an active role . . . that we can prevent the social care voice from being subsumed by the behemoth that is the NHS. (Dr Nick Hervey, Social Care Lead, South London and Maudsley Foundation NHS Trust)

The model in Figure 5.2 maintains discrete management functions between health provision and social care provision which extents down to front line team manager level.

The benefit here is that each area has the opportunity to develop its own strategy direction and leadership structures, without relying on another discipline or organisation to ensure delivery. While at strategic and management levels this has a number of benefits, for the staff on the ground it can often be confusing and conflicting, with the phenomenon of 'too many chiefs' evident throughout the services that have implemented this approach.

In addition, the integration agenda is only being delivered on the ground within this model, and areas such as joint commissioning, strategic direction and the development of shared visions and goals between organisations are not achievable within this structure.

Figure 5.2: Possible management structures 2

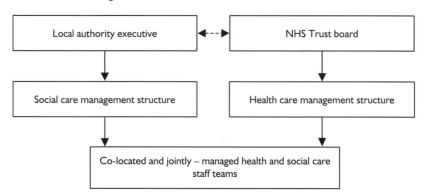

Figure 5.3: Possible management structures 3

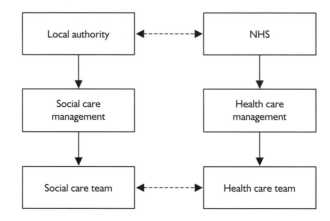

The final service configuration shown in Figure 5.3 retains independent management and accountability between health and social care, with linkage occurring both strategically and at the front line of provision, with teams often co-located. This model is the one that offers the path of least resistance in terms of radical change, as both leaders and practitioners are familiar with the issues of cooperation and joint working. Within this structure no radical organisational change, which can often lead to upheaval and disruption, is required in order to ensure implementation.

In real terms the co-location of staff is not a fully integrated provision and there remain conflicts between health and social care that are not easily resolved within this structure. These can include key performance targets and the discrepancies between resource allocations within different areas. As Tony, a social worker, commented:

> *Health staff can see beyond the medical model and social work staff are not solely reliant on the social model. But any small divisions are likely to be heightened in times of scarce resources. If the finances were plentiful people would be only too happy to share their time and resources.* (Tony, social worker)

None of these models is without its drawbacks, but in many cases there has been a reluctance on behalf of both health and social care organisations to commit to full integration of services, under a single structure, with disciplines often seeing such a move as an attack on their professional identity, and losing sight of the reasons for the existence of their chosen profession in the first place.

> *I am still unpleasantly surprised when care professionals (and I've chosen this word deliberately!) still perceive to be on different sides – we should all be on the same side: that of the person receiving a service!* (Emmy, health and social care worker)

This situation is further compounded, on both an organisational and strategic level, by the influence of segregated regulatory systems (as discussed elsewhere), which specify different key indicators and separate statutory criteria, and place different duties on health and social care organisations.

Reflection point

Which model do you feel would be the most effective to implement within your area?

Human resource considerations

In 2005 the Integrated Care Network (ICN) issued a paper to help organisations to implement the integration agenda. Part of this paper concentrated upon the human resource issues and challenges involved in bringing together two groups of staff. These were as follows:

- employees are entitled to be treated in accordance with their 'home' terms and conditions;

- legal arrangements under employment legislation mean that contractual policy arrangements must be retained;

- busy managers may find it difficult to understand the implications of having employees from more than one organisation, who have different entitlements, and supported by different policy and procedural arrangements.

(ICN and CSIP, 2005, p. 33)

These are significant issues within the debate. As roles within mental health services are becoming more generic, with core capabilities (such as the Essential Shared Capabilities and Capable Practitioner requirements discussed in detail in Chapter 3) being implemented across disciplines, the discrepancies between terms, conditions and salary scales between NHS bodies and local authority organisations are being highlighted to a greater degree.

In some areas this is leading to a difficulty in terms of recruitment and retention of staff. The NHS Agenda 4 Change pay review has served to standardise pay and conditions within health organisations, but local authorities are yet to achieve the same standardisation, and different areas are able to attach differing bonuses to their terms and conditions of service. With social care staff being seconded into NHS organisations on protected pay, many professionals are finding it difficult to move employment within their new health hosts. Team manager scales, for example, in local authorities are paid at a significantly higher level than their health colleagues, and staff are therefore unwilling to sacrifice their protection to take on new employment challenges. Likewise, when new social care posts are established employment is often directly by the health authority, with the Agenda 4 Change scales attached, and as a result posts are difficult to fill because the rate of remuneration is not comparable to local authority employers. With social care staff already suspicious with regard to being employed by an NHS body, this situation is not facilitating the development of the social care workforce within mental health services.

Organisational accountability structures

When considering the integration of health and social care, we are in fact dealing with two distinct cultures and structures that have little in terms of structural common ground. While the aims of the 2006 white paper *OHOCOS* are not in debate in terms of providing joined up and seamless services, the reality of these aims are complex due to the cultural make up of the stakeholders. These differences were discussed by Rowden in 2005, who stated:

> NHS boards are appointed, not elected, and are accountable to central government. By contrast, in local authorities, elected local councillors are in charge, with council staff then accountable to the community through them . . . While social services directors and senior managers accept public political scrutiny by councillors on a regular basis, NHS chief executive officers and senior managers have nothing like this level of scrutiny and accountability to the local community. (Rowden, 2005)

The ability to reconcile these accountability arrangements on an organisational level is essential if truly integrated services are to be developed. However, rather than becoming more aligned, the NHS is moving more towards a market model with the introduction of foundation trusts, an aspect which is creating anxiety among local authority partners.

Governance structures

All organisations providing public services are required to have an identified governance structure, which allows for clear accountability and quality assurance to be put into place. The nature and focus of this structure can, and does, differ across individual trusts within the NHS, although common areas are required, specified as:

- patient safety, including health and safety and risk management
- quality, including clinical governance arrangements
- resources, including financial management
- responsibilities, including management structures.

In the case of local government social services departments, the framework for governance is standardised with the framework developed by CIPFA/SOLICE (2007), which defines governance as:

> about how local government bodies ensure that they are doing the right things, in the right way, for the right people in a timely, inclusive, open, honest and accountable manner. It comprises the systems and processes for the direction and control of local authorities through which they account to, engage with and lead their communities.

With five clear domains identified as requiring robust governance arrangements, these are:

- community focus, including involvement, representation and public opinion

- service delivery, including quality assurance, accessibility and responsiveness to local community needs

- structure and process, including management structures and care pathways

- risk management and internal control, including health and safety

- standards of conduct, including application of professional standards.

While these two structures are not diametrically opposed, there is enough difference to create both myth and misunderstanding, especially where one organisation is carrying the delegated responsibility for the delivery of the other services.

The requirement for community focus and accountability is the most problematic area that faces NHS Trusts with social services responsibility, because while they are required to develop involvement and public representation mechanisms, there remains a clear distinction between accountability to government and direct accountability to the voting public for service delivery that is not easily reconciled within the governance arrangements.

NHS Trusts are by their very nature hierarchical cultures, in which reporting and monitoring systems are created to inform board level decisions that are largely dictated by the Department of Health and national NHS standards and regulators.

Local authorities, by contrast, have far more freedoms in terms of central government control, but are directly answerable to the communities they serve, and as a result their operation is traditionally more consultative and inclusive in its nature.

These cultural discrepancies are evident throughout the two types of organisations, and governance structures within integrated trusts have a tendency to be health-led, and may therefore overlook, or misunderstand, the local authority requirements.

This can then result in local authorities expressing concerns regarding how effective the NHS can be, in terms of the delivery and governance of social services responsibilities. The fact that the accountability for social care services remains with the local authority creates a range of anxieties for both organisations, and partnership arrangements can be fraught with suspicion and defensiveness if both partners are not clear about responsibilities for quality and standards from the outset of agreed arrangements.

Reflection points

To what extent have local services in your area achieved linkage between accountability and governance arrangements?

What would assist the NHS and social care organisations to reconcile their differences in this regard, where staff are seconded to NHS organisations?

Impact of secondment on staff

For social care staff who have been seconded into NHS services, there exist a number of issues. They remain employees of the local authority, but become operationally responsible to an external organisation, one in which they are often the isolated voice in terms of both the social model and the statutory duties they are required to uphold as accountable professionals.

The retention of their employment terms and conditions, while ensuring their protection under employment law, gives rise to confusion when procedures are required (for example grievance and disciplinary issues), and in many cases local authorities, while required to identify a lead manager for mental health commissioning, have not retained a mental health specialist who is able to provide for their professional and organisational needs.

The new organisational culture that they are required to work within can appear alien and unfamiliar, with an emphasis on medically driven approaches and consultant-led service provision that does not cater for their practice in terms of legislative frameworks or developmental needs.

Morale is often an issue within organisations that have applied the secondment model of integration, with a lack of ownership and support from their employing authority, and a lack of understanding and appreciation of the social care role or social model within the host organisation:

> as social care workers we are often isolated in our teams. Certainly, being the lone voice shouting the social perspective is common throughout my experiences.
> (Steve, social worker)

While there are exceptions, many seconded workers therefore find themselves 'cut loose', with little in terms of structure to support what is often a complex and challenging workload.

Impact of secondment on quality assurance

Research across a range of disciplines and environments, concerning the impact of worker morale on the quality of service delivery, is particularly relevant at this point in the discussion (Pollitt, 1990; Smith, 1992; Harvey and Kitson, 1996; Desombre and Eccles,1998; Carey, 2003; Currie et al., 2005).

There is significant evidence to suggest that an unhappy workforce has a direct impact upon the quality of care, and this alone is sufficient to raise concerns regarding service delivery. The difficulties in aligning human resources, management structures and governance arrangements, as well as differing organisational cultures, all require some attention. These are the systems by which organisations are able to benchmark the services they provide, and without which focus and quality of provision remain difficult to determine and interpret.

Despite the apparent difficulties and concerns, the social services input into mental health services and the integrative philosophy remain consistently agreed, and while a range of issues still needs to be resolved, progress is being made across the country to promote the principle of a 'seamless journey' through services, which prior to integration had not been possible.

While this chapter has highlighted areas of conflict as a general theme, this does not detract from the progress that has been made to varying degrees and varying levels within seconded and delegated authority organisations. There are key examples of innovative and good practice initiatives being delivered within partnership frameworks across the country. In order to illustrate this point, and provide a counter-balance to the previous discussions, Figure 5.4 describes a number of good practice partnership examples that have been highlighted within mental health services, and where secondment has been the preferred model of service delivery.

Many further local examples of partnerships at work within communities and services could have been detailed here to illustrate some of the potential benefits of integrated provision for those who require support from services. The examples included demonstrate that improvements can be achieved via a range of mechanisms, from front line service delivery to research and strategic direction.

Reflection point

What are the examples of good practice partnership and integration, where service users have benefited from service improvements as a result, within your local area?

Figure 5.4: Case study examples – good practice in partnerships

Cornwall: Support Time and Recovery (STR) Workers within the NHS trust have been supported to actively promote social inclusion links. They have given three people surfing lessons and bought them equipment. These were people for whom traditional services did nothing, and needed something specifically for them.

Waltham Forest: Established a performance clinic, which has a rolling programme of review events focusing on a particular target, issue or service. The programme includes wide organisational and community involvement, including members, front line staff, relevant partners and users. A senior officer produces an action plan, which is monitored as part of wider performance management processes.

Birmingham: The Transforming Lives; Changing Services project is being undertaken by Sure-search, a research and training network of service users and their allies, based at Birmingham University (Davis and Braithwaite, 2001). Following the conclusion of this research, Sure-search members, who are service users, are now working on selected service sites with service users and staff, using service user-generated criteria as a basis to evaluate the existing service and stimulate exchanges between staff and service users about what needs to change in order to make services more responsive to users' needs.

Is it a question of ownership?

This chapter began with a quote from Bob Nelson, who believes that the productiveness of employees is directly influenced by their interaction with their managers. From this discussion, it is possible to suggest that this premise is also the case within health and social care services.

The distinct nature of public service provision, and of social care itself, is that the impact of the interaction is not confined to the individual worker's line manager or management structure, but affects a wider system comprising strategy, governance, culture and community interaction.

Social workers are not new to the idea of systems theory and how each component part has an influence on the others, and it is therefore not surprising that wider conflicts and challenges can affect worker morale, professional identity (as discussed in Chapter 3) and hence quality assurance across mental health services as a whole.

Secondment and delegation of duties, without the loss of employment status and other controls, have the benefit of retaining the social workers' connection to their authority (and hence the statutory framework and overall understanding of the social care model of delivery); however, they can also create difficulties in terms of who owns the provision, the workforce and the requirements of the service. This can result in isolation and disconnection by the workforce and an inability on the part of host organisations to apply performance management and robust accountability arrangements within their operational management systems that meet the needs of social care workers or service users.

In order to apply this model of integration successfully, clear responsibility needs to be established and the range of structures in both the NHS and local authorities requires reconciliation to ensure that service delivery meets the standards of high quality, 'safe sound and supportive' (DoH, 1998a) service delivery across the sector. The full integration of services, while attempting to address the ownership issues, does give rise to a range of other challenges, and these will be examined and discussed in Chapter 6.

Further reading

Integrated Care Network and CSIP (2005) *Bringing the NHS and Local Government Together: Integrating the Workforce, A Guide*. London: ICN.

Social Perspectives Network (2004) *Integration of Health and Social Care: Promoting Social Care Perspectives Within Integrated Mental Health Services*. SPN Paper 6.

Chaper 6
Wholesale change?

It takes a lot of courage to release the familiar and seemingly secure, to embrace the new. But there is no real security in what is no longer meaningful. There is more security in the adventurous and exciting, for in movement there is life, and in change there is power.
(Alan Cohen, US author)

PQ framework

Achieving Post-qualifying Social Work awards

This chapter will assist in the meeting of National Occupational Standards for Social Work:

Key Role 5, Unit 17:   Work within multi-disciplinary and multi-organisational teams, networks and systems.

Key Role 6, Unit 21:   Contribute to the promotion of best social work practice.

For registered social workers considering, or working towards, post-qualifying awards this chapter will also assist in meeting the requirements of both the specialist award in mental health, and the national occupational standards in mental health, which are core to the post-qualification standards in this area.

MHNOS 67:   Encourage stakeholders to see the value of improving environments and practices to promote mental health.

MHNOS 79:   Enable workers and agencies to work collaboratively.

PQ Specialist Award in Mental Health

47 (vii)   Working collaboratively with other professions; promoting the social model of need/disability/mental health within multidisciplinary settings.

47 (xi)   Influencing and supporting communities, organisations, agencies and services to promote people's mental health.

Introduction

In Chapter 5 the partial transfer of duties, via secondment arrangements, was discussed and the implications in terms of governance, accountability and organisational culture were highlighted as considerations of the approach. There are, however, a range of integrative models that have been adopted by organisations and this chapter seeks to examine the implications of wholesale change, where staff and duties are fully owned by the host organisation, with employment transfers and operational accountability located within the core business delivery of the NHS. This chapter explores the impact of this approach on staff, morale and ultimately service delivery, and asks what the benefits and potential costs are of these arrangements.

Mental health services and social care services are current facing two driving forces. On the one hand, the introduction of *New Ways of Working for Everyone* (DoH, 2007a) is introducing an expansion of roles, team capabilities and an inter-professional workforce. On the other hand, *Transforming Social Care* (DoH, 2008) is due to commence the implementation of the personalisation agenda, with advocacy and brokerage rather than assessment and gate keeping being the emphasis for the future of care delivery. The social care workforce operating within the NHS is potentially facing a conflict in the implementation of the modernisation agenda, and as with integration overall, the challenge will be to reconcile the competing cultures of health and social care service delivery.

The meaning and purpose of integration

As already discussed within previous chapters, the integration of health and social care constitutes a significant driver in the government's agenda for modernising service provision across the sector, with the overall aim of providing joined-up care for those most in need within the community. There is, however, substantial scepticism about the willingness and ability of health and social care professionals to engage fully in the integration process (Hudson, 2002), and as a result it is likely that the organisational ability to take on the agenda will be impaired.

It is perhaps useful at this point in the debate to outline what is meant by the term 'integration'. It can be used to describe a number of circumstances, as Kharicha et al. (2004) commented in regard to integrated services:

> *there is little consensus about what it means in practice. It can refer to autonomous professionals exchanging views and information; fully or partly co-located multidisciplinary joint and team working; inter-disciplinary collaboration across organisational boundaries and structures; or shared governance structures and joint control of human and financial resource decision making.* (Cited in Social Care Institute for Excellence, 2005, p. 11)

For the purposes of this discussion, full integration is defined as shared governance and management structures, located in one organisation. Single lines of accountability and responsibility, which link to the local authority via partnership management boards which lead the strategic direction and performance management requirements, maintain the arrangements. Operational responsibility is delivered within a single structure, with the purpose being to bring together

> *inputs, delivery, management and organisation of services as a means [of] improving access, quality, user satisfaction and efficiency.* (Gröne and Garcia-Barbero, 2001, p. 7)

This process began with the application of the Health Act 1999 flexibilities (superseded by section 75 of the NHS Act 2006), which was followed by a range of health and social care guidance and policy aiming to align the delivery frameworks, and most recently the key aims of the 2006 white paper, *Our Health, Our Care, Our Say*, further strengthening the direction of travel with key aims for service delivery specified. Figure 6.1 illustrates these goals, which are to be applied across all health and social care services.

The application of these strategic aims is possible within mental health care, but the understanding of what each may mean, and how they are to be delivered, is an area that needs some clarification. The focus of *New Ways of Working* is to deliver key evidence-based psychosocial interventions from within multi-professional teams, whereas the focus of transforming social care is to allocate personal budgets for service users to purchase the care they require to improve the overall quality of life. The emphasis in both of these foci is person-centred support, but how this is delivered is potentially a significant contrast. As a result the method by which social care staff, operating within mental health services, take forward these agendas is still an area of uncertainty. An additional consideration in this discussion is the fact that the lead agency for each agenda is different, which begs the question whether the NHS has a sufficient understanding of the requirements of transforming social care to be able to deliver on behalf of its local authority partners.

Reflection point

Does the joining up of health and social care services lead to equality of access?

Defining boundaries

It is recognised that the boundary between health care and social care has become less than clear over the last decade, and professionals from both sides of the divide are becoming more adept at identifying needs in a more holistic manner. This is supported by initiatives such as *Essential Shared Capabilities* and *New Ways of Working*, and the subsequent *Creating Capable Teams* (CSIP, 2008) which concentrates on the development of multi-disciplinary

Figure 6.1: Strategic goals of Our Health, Our Care, Our Say

- Better prevention services and early intervention
- More choice and a louder voice
- Tackling inequality and improved access to community services
- More support for people with long-term needs.

---

teams), and so it would not be a huge leap to suggest that service integration would be a logical next step. However, the alignment of organisations and regulatory systems is still some way behind that of the policy framework, and a range of challenges remain as yet unresolved.

Health Act flexibilities – the impact of partnership trusts

Chapter 1 provided the background and a detailed discussion regarding the application of section 31 agreements. Nationally a range of organisations have entered into such arrangements, with PCTs and local authorities applying the flexibilities to enable joint commissioning arrangements, and local authorities and NHS Trusts developing partnership arrangements for the direct delivery of health and social care services. In mental health terms, a number of NHS partnership trusts were founded by merging the previous community mental health trusts with the social services provision for this service user group. This has variously included community-based care, approved social work services, and social care support services.

For those areas that opted for the full integration model, the aim was to merge health and social care into a single coherent organisational structure. The disparities between budgets, key performance indicators and access arrangements have meant that this step was not as straightforward as initially considered. The policy framework around health and social care, as well as the amendments associated with mental health legislation, have continued to develop and previously unconsidered issues have come to light after agreements were made which have resulted in the need for constant review and revision, something which in some areas has not been effectively applied.

NHS responsibility versus local authority accountability

The provision of Approved Social Worker (ASW) services is a key example of the difficulties involved in NHS services delivering social services responsibilities (see Chapter 10 for further discussion on this issue). Under the Mental Health Act 1983, local authorities are required to ensure the 'sufficiency' (s114) of ASW staff for the local population, and the accountability for the practice of ASWs remains a statutory obligation for local authorities.

This is a challenge for all parties in areas where full integration, and hence the transfer of staff to the NHS, have occurred. In these circumstances the local authorities do not employ ASWs and as a result the NHS has delegated operational responsibility for the service. This position is one of anxiety for all those involved. The NHS has traditionally not considered the service to be part of its core business, and so while it holds delegated responsibility the service does not receive the priority in an environment of increasing workload pressures. As a result ASW staff can find themselves with a range of demands being placed upon them by both operational managers and those in the NHS organisation who are tasked with delivering the ASW service provision. In a climate of an ageing workforce and ever decreasing numbers of qualified and competent ASWs to deliver the service, those on the front line often face isolation and challenge from other professions when they are attempting to balance team responsibilities and statutory responsibilities, within an organisation that may not fully understand the implications of their dual roles.

This is not a new phenomenon, and it is possible that ASWs within local authorities faced the same types of challenges. However, while local authority employers were obliged to provide a sufficient service, the NHS is providing it via delegated responsibility, and as a result the buck does not stop with the operational management in the same way as it does within social services departments. In addition to this consideration, local authorities are also distancing themselves from the provision of mental health services in a manner which historically they have been unable to do. As the NHS takes over organisational responsibility, local authorities are under less pressure to provide staff from outside the mental health services. In previous years it was not uncommon to have ASW staff from other sectors, such as learning disabilities and child care, but this is now become less common and managers within these services are able to prevent their qualified staff from engaging in rota duties by stating that the service capacity does not allow for that individual's release from team duties. This leaves little in terms of redress for the NHS organisation that is required to deliver the service.

Independence of the ASW role was a significant consideration for professionals when integration of health and social care was first initiated, and this debate has remained. The introduction of the Approved Mental Health Professional (AMHP) role will be discussed further in Chapter 10, but it is worth noting at this point that there was significant concern from the ASW workforce, in the first instance, regarding how independent the role would remain if ASW staff were directly employed by the NHS. For those who have become NHS employees, this issue, while a consideration, has not become an issue on the expected scale. Part of the reason for this is the discrete legal status held by an ASW, and also local authority retention of accountability for ASW practice. The lack of understanding by NHS managers has assisted in the retention of the independence of the role, as few professionals outside social work have a clear understanding of the functions, powers and duties that an ASW exercises. This situation may change in the future, but at this time there appears to be no evidence that the original concerns regarding erosion of the role have actually occurred in practice.

Ownership implications

The example of the ASW role is just one of the possible scenarios facing organisations and staff within partnership arrangements. Other services within the realms of social care (such as safeguarding adults, continuing professional development, and social care funding) are all subject to the same types of pressures, with section 31/75 agreements in place that require the NHS to deliver a service that it is not fully accountable for, and enable local authorities to distance themselves from that provision as they are not responsible for its delivery. In most circumstances the front line staff and managers are the individuals left in a pressurised situation, with no real ownership from either party creating a feeling of insecurity and isolation, and a general lack of organisational support. This situation contributes not only to the quality of the service but also to the morale and competency of the workforce tasked to deliver the arrangements within unclear boundaries.

> ## Reflection point
>
> Consider your own work setting – what is the impact of boundaries on your professional practice?

In some organisations which have been able to achieve a balanced management structure between health and social care professionals, and strong partnership arrangements, the challenges of responsibility and accountability being located in separate organisations has been less of a issue. However, the discrepancy in size and volume between the NHS health-led services and social services provision in the field has made this a difficult position to achieve, and many local authorities have chosen not to retain any mental health expertise to support the transferred staff or services.

Different cultures – different languages?

Chapter 5 highlighted the differences in management structure and organisational culture as key issues for seconded staff. It can be argued that these differences are more acute for partnership trusts that have taken on social care in a more wholesale manner. Whereas secondment allows for a link to remain with employing organisations, transferred staff do not have those same links and can find themselves operating within an alien culture, with hierarchical, medically driven structures being the norm. This shift is one that social care staff and services often find difficult, and can add to the feeling of isolation and uncertainty that social workers, in particular, experience. In the case of Community Mental Health Teams (CMHT), social workers are often in the minority, with one or two social workers to many community psychiatric nurses (CPNs), and often a manager with a health care background. While attempts to provide professional support have been made with a senior social worker often located within these teams, the disparity in numbers alone creates a culture that is health dominated and within which social care is often a lone voice.

Professional structures

The difference in professional structures and terminology between health staff and social care staff is an area that has caused some misconceptions. Health staff tend to refer to their work as clinical, whereas social care workers refer to practice as the core activity. Areas such as supervision, professional accountability and line management are all areas in which discrepancies are apparent. Figure 6.2 illustrates some of these key differences.

Medical staff have traditionally been aligned to their clinical and medical directors, and linked into specific teams or service areas; psychology staff operate a similar framework. Nurses have a culture of separated management and clinical supervision and social workers have historically combined management and practice supervision into a single framework. These differences are key issues in terms of professional understanding of operating structures, and can create uncertainly among staff in terms of where their responsibilities and accountabilities lie when attempting to align organisational cultures.

Figure 6.2: Differences in professional structures

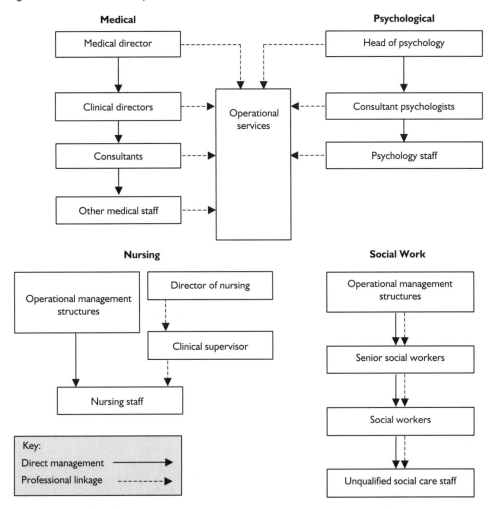

The multi-professional nature of the NHS, as opposed to the historically uni-professional nature of social services departments, is a contributory factor to these differences in structure and cultures. While it is argued that the NHS has been medically dominated, the other health and allied health professionals within the services have played a key role and as such have developed professional structures to support clinical work. Social work and social care, on the other hand, while linking outside the employing agency to a range of statutory, private and voluntary sector organisations, have had a commonality of professional approach within the employing organisation, and as such the development of professional accountability has successfully remained within the overall management structures.

The integration of health and social care services has had the greatest impact upon social care in terms of professional structures, as for the first time statutory sector social workers have found themselves managed by individuals and structures that are unfamiliar with their roles, duties and perspectives. This has necessitated the development of lines of professional accountability alongside line management arrangements. This situation has been a difficult shift for social care professionals and health care managers alike, as each group has been required to participate in a system that is unfamiliar, with little in the way of induction for, or awareness of, the customs and functions of each professional group.

In an environment that represents cultural competence as a key professional skill it is possible to suggest that the same consideration has not been given to the workers tasked to deliver the services. This omission has led to some difficulties in terms of merging professional structures and accountabilities.

Change management – an organisational skill

Over the past twenty years a significant amount of research has been carried out within the realms of organisational change (Mintzberg, 1989; Gladwell, 2000; Kotter, 1995; Weick and Quinn, 1999; Stacey, 1996) and the impact that these changes have on the individuals and groups that inhabit those organisations. Both the NHS and local authorities have made substantial investment in restructuring and promoting leadership within their departments. This has the ultimate aim of improving efficiency and effectiveness of the systems of service delivery, and hence improving service user outcomes.

Change in organisations involves three distinct yet connected areas – the people, the culture and the processes. The integration agenda has involved a large scale change for all those involved; this is especially the case for agencies that opted to directly transfer staff and duties, such as partnership trusts. For these changes to be successful attention to all three areas is required, but in many cases this has not been the case. As a result staff and organisations are left feeling vulnerable and unsure of the roles, functions and purpose of what can feel like an endless cycle of restructuring and change.

The people

This includes the whole range of staff, from senior managers to front line practitioners, administrative and support staff. Essentially, service users and carers, advocacy groups and voluntary and private sector partners all need to be involved, consulted and considered, and it is necessary to ensure that any change is both explained and objectively balanced. Change for change's sake is an accusation that is often levelled at the statutory sector, and in an environment of increasing market competition, the necessity to provide a rationale and be accountable for change is increasing. In order effectively to manage and lead any change it is necessary to consider two key questions – who are the stakeholders in this process, and what outcomes are to be achieved by making the change? Integration, while ultimately directed by the policy framework, is not excluded from these considerations and local interpretation needs to ensure that the people involved are sufficiently prepared and engaged in the process.

The culture

All groups have a cultural element, and organisations such as health and social care providers are all types of group with a series of cultures. The identification of professionals with both their profession and their employing bodies was discussed in detail in Chapter 3; however, those points are equally valid here.

The integration of services has failed fully to consider the cultural elements of each of the professions in its attempt to join up health and social care. This joining up cannot be achieved by simple co-location or singularity in management; recognition of each professional group and what it brings in terms of experience, custom and practice is required within the process. In dealing with any change, significant consideration and time are required. There is a necessity to engage with each group, and to identify power relationships that can be used to drive forward the change process. As with the people element, the culture element can often be neglected or not become evident until a clash or resistance from a particular faction is evident, a stage at which the effectiveness of the planned change may have already been compromised.

The process

The actual process by which change occurs is the area that most organisations are most eager to address. The detail of what is proposed, how it will develop and be implemented, and how it will be monitored and evaluated, are all areas that are familiar to the management agenda as they form the key elements of daily business. The process is a vital element in any change, as a plan of action is what maintains the boundaries and expectations of any change process. However, the failing of many managers and leaders is the over-concentration on process to the exclusion of the human elements (people and culture), and the presumption that creating a process will necessitate the change. It is often the case that change processes are resisted, challenged and sabotaged by individuals and groups within the systems, and the personal and professional power of organisational members cannot be overestimated as these have the potential to either drive or stonewall any given change process. Integration of services is a key example of this phenomenon. Where consultation has occurred with professional groups, unions and other stakeholders, the transfer process has been more successful both in terms of its implementation and its maintenance.

In large bureaucratic organisations, such as the NHS and local authorities, the emphasis is too often placed upon process and policy, with an assumption that if these things are in place the other elements will follow. However, as discussed, this is not the case, and regardless of how much attention is paid to detailed systems and process mapping, the impact upon staff at the front line, and ultimately the users of services, is key to the deliverable success of any change process. Without people and culture change the consequences of change will be far greater than the benefits.

Whole systems and the NHS

Within the NHS the term 'whole systems' is one with which staff at all levels of the organisation will be familiar, but it appears from a social care perspective that this emphasis has been somewhat lacking throughout the integrative experience. While a whole-systems approach has been applied to service improvement and working towards the aims of 'joined-up' and 'seamless' provision, the achievement of this goal has not seen the same approach. Partnership arrangements across the country have been variable, in both their detail and their appreciation of the future direction of social care. Key issues, such as development of a shared vision, are in some cases still to be achieved, and while there is agreement on the emphasis upon person-centred care, what this actually means and how it is interpreted in terms of service structure and implementation has huge variability. It appears that this is often dependent upon local political, media and public views, rather than an objective evidence-based stance.

Reflection point

To what extent has your agency considered the three essential elements – people, culture and process – when making changes?

What impact has the organisational emphasis had upon your practice and position?

Is integration a wholesale change?

This chapter started with a quote from Alan Cohen discussing the two sides of any change: on the one hand, moving away from what is known is a fearful experience that requires courage to undertake; and on the other hand, to remain in a situation that is meaningless or is not able to meet the individual or organisational needs can be a destructive action that inhibits growth. In integration terms this analysis is appropriate: the direction of travel is to join up services and move towards a health and social care provision that does not attempt to apply demarcations upon which needs or which services fit within which definition. This shift is one which professionals and agencies are experiencing key changes on both physical and psychological levels. Social workers have seen changes in their employing bodies, changes within the management structures in which they work, changes in their overall roles and functions, and to a certain extent, changes in the application of their professional perspectives. All these changes are based upon hierarchical decisions made at central government level, whereby workers are told what the future of social care is to be, rather than consulted and invited to join the discussions of what it might be.

This is an anxiety-provoking situation for social care staff. The emphasis on process within the Health Act flexibilities has created a situation in which the human element of integration is considered far less of a priority than the detail within which the partnership arrangements are delivered. As a result, fully transferred staff are often finding it difficult to adapt to their new environments which can result in disempowerment and de-skilling of professionals. This is a situation that can, and does, have a direct impact upon the quality and effectiveness of the care delivery.

As with Chapter 5, this chapter has discussed a range of considerations and potential challenges that face organisations when entering into the wholesale change that partnership arrangements and transfer of staff and duties require. This debate is one in which there are key positives: the notion of seamless, integrated and joined-up services that provide accessibility and high quality provision is not under question here, and these issues do not seek to present an argument contrary to the integration agenda.

The overall concepts, context and nature of integration are supported throughout both this chapter and the overall text. As social care professionals, the arts of critical appraisal and reflection are viewed as essential learning tools and it is necessary, throughout the process, to question and present challenges to these initiatives. By doing so workers will be better able to understand fully the implications on those individuals, groups and communities that professions and services are ultimately accountable to – the users of the services provided.

Further reading

Gröne, O. and Garcia-Barbero, M. (2001) Integrated care: a position paper of the WHO European Office for Integrated Health Care Services. *International Journal of Integrated Care*, 1; (1). Available at: www.ijic.org

Iles, V. and Sutherland, K. (2006) *Managing Change in the NHS: Organisation Change, a Review for Health Care Managers, Professionals and Researchers*. London: NCC/SDO.

Chapter 7
Working in partnership

'If we are together nothing is impossible, if we are divided all will fail.'
(Winston Churchill, 1874–1965)

PQ framework

Achieving Post-qualifying Social Work awards

This chapter will assist in evidencing the National Occupational Standards for Social Work:

Key Role 5, Unit 17: Work within multi-disciplinary and multi-organisational teams, networks and systems.

Key Role 6, Unit 18: Research, analyse, evaluate, and use current knowledge of best social work practice

For registered social workers considering, or working towards, post-qualification awards, this chapter will also assist in meeting the requirements of both the specialist award in mental health, and the national occupational standards in mental health, which are core to the post-qualifying standards in this area.

MHNOS 80: Explore, initiate and develop collaborative working relationships.

MHNOS 86: Monitor, evaluate and improve inter-agency services for addressing mental health needs.

PQ Specialist Award in Mental Health

47 (vii) Working collaboratively with other professions; promoting the social model of need/disability/mental health within multidisciplinary settings.

47 (x) Utilising appropriate knowledge and research from other disciplines.

Introduction

The Health Act 1999 (see Chapter 1 for full details) gave health and social care authorities the option of joining up both the commissioning processes and direct provisions. The aim was to create a range of services whose delivery was more efficient and cost effective. The drive for service improvement had indicated that the gap (and duplication) between services and the lack of integration was contributing to some failings, both in terms of the application of 'best value' and also in terms of delivering quality services that were able to meet local need.

In common law the term 'partnership' refers to a type of business entity in which partners share with each other the profits or losses of the business undertaking in which they have invested. In terms of the NHS and social services provision in this country, can this definition by applied, or is it necessary to define the partnership arrangements under a separate set of criteria to that of businesses?

The push towards foundation trust status within the NHS places health bodies in a business environment. However, as social services operate according to local community and governmental requirements rather than business requirements, are the two agendas compatible? Can true partnerships be achieved while there is an imbalance in terms of organisational cultures, goals and driving agendas?

This chapter looks at the notion and theory of partnership working, as defined by the Health Act 1999 and subsequent policy guidance, and asks whether true partnership is achievable between health and social care commissioners and providers in the practice environment.

Partnership theory

In order to begin to evaluate the success, or otherwise, of partnership models within mental health services, it is necessary to have an understanding of the definitions and theoretical underpinnings that govern these developments. This chapter does not seek to be a comprehensive guide to partnership theory, and readers are directed to the reading list provided by the King's Fund for full details of the reports and research in this area (King's Fund, 2006).

When considering partnership between public sector organisations it is beneficial to have an insight into two particular theories of partnership – the open-systems model and the institutional model. Each has a framework to offer which can inform critical thinking and evaluation of the current integrated environment.

Open-systems theory

Systems theory is not a new model for social workers as it is one of the key approaches taught at diploma and undergraduate levels. Open-systems theory is based on general systems thinking, focusing on dynamic and reoccurring interactions between people, environments and cultures.

Within this perspective partnership is viewed as a social system, with a range of sub-systems that interact with each other and their environments (Katz and Kahn, 1978). It proposes that systems maintain themselves via environmental contact and defines partnership arrangements as:

> *a coalition of shifting interest groups, strongly influenced by environmental factors that develop goals by negotiating its structure, activity and outcomes.*
> (Adapted from Katz and Kahn, 1978)

The theory suggests that there is a requirement for five sub-systems within any partnership, without which the survival of the arrangement is not viable (Scott, 1992):

1. Production/technical structures

2. Boundary spanning structures

3. Maintenance structures

4. Adaptive structures

5. Managerial structures.

Each sub-system has a role within the partnership, in terms of ensuring that the overall system is working towards the shared goal. Figure 7.1 considers these sub-systems as applied to health and social care partnership arrangements within mental health.

Within the mental health service provision the technical aspects of care are often central, and professional power relationships and the specialist nature of the care provided (as discussed in previous chapters) maintain this centrality. The ethos of person-centred care will retain this position; this is because regardless of the other structures, the basic principle of mental health services is to provide quality care to those in need.

This creates a situation whereby sub-systems other than those of a technical, care delivery-based, nature are seen as less important or supplementary by the professionals within the system rather than essential to the delivery of the partnership aims and goals.

This premise supports the view that within the sub-systems there may be a wide complexity and variability of the organisational parts and functions. This leads to a looseness of connections between each system which can lead to shifting boundaries, and a tendency to focus

Figure 7.1: Health and social care partnership sub-systems

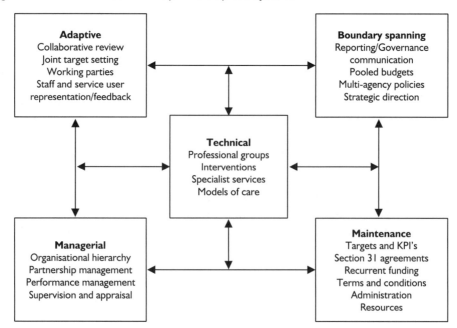

on process rather than structure (Scott, 1992). For a large organisation such as a mental health partnership trust this is a difficult system to sustain, and each sub-system will exert its own influence dependent upon its particular agenda. This can cause a high degree of conflict and fragmentation within the organisation, if not carefully managed.

Reflection point

To what extent do the connections between internal systems affect the delivery of care in your organisation?

Is there any difference between the systems within health and with social care organisations that could affect the way the systems interact?

Criticisms of open-systems theory

The main criticism of this theoretical approach is that it views the organisation solely as a physical entity, and as such ignores the human element (Flood, 1999). This can have a significant impact upon the success or failure of any given partnership within the sector.

With this criticism in mind, the second theory for consideration is that of the institutional perspective, which while based upon the open-systems approach provides further development, and thus is more easily applicable to health and social service organisations.

Institutional theory

Institutional approaches consider environment to be more than a stock of resources and information, and as a result the system expands beyond the internal and into the external as a supplier of legitimacy and meaning (Thompson, 1967). A whole range of environmental factors can have a significant impact upon any given system; in the mental health field, issues such as regulatory and inspection frameworks, statutory duties and other organisational agendas can all serve to either stabilise or destabilise the system, and can define whether a given partnership is considered a success. This increase in environmental complexity and demand has the potential to create a higher level of organisational interdependence than that described within open-systems approaches (Scott, 1992), as each system strives towards coordination for the purposes of sustaining its own position.

Within this model there are four elements, in addition to the internal sub-systems already described within the open-systems approaches, which can exert varying levels of influence over the system (adapted from Scott and Meyer, 1994):

1. macro-processes in power and social structures that affect and control the development of any given environment;

2. institutional environments made up of sets of organisations with individual identities, structures and activities;

3. casual connections that can influence particular organisations;

4. sources of influence outside organisational structures.

This approach is considered to be more appropriate to the context of health and social care partnerships, as while organisations have been created to house partnership arrangements, these are still subject to a range of pressures and forces outside the created organisation. Each of these influences has the potential to have a direct impact upon the partnership viability.

Figure 7.2 illustrates the institutional model as applied to mental health service partnerships. This model of partnership is more representative of the current system within mental health services. Partnerships made under the 1999 Health Act are subject to a whole range of influences from the environment in which they operate, and these have the potential to shape services as significantly as the internal organisational sub-systems.

A further consideration within this model is that a distinction is made between two types of organisations (DiMaggio and Powell, 1991), these being:

● technical – dependent upon output (including profits);

● institutional – dependent upon acceptance of social norms and values.

Partnership trusts are in fact attempting to create a third type of organisation, which is supported by the drive for best value and efficiency across health and social care services. The partnership arrangements are attempting to combine the technical and production-driven service delivery which is also within the realms of social norms and values.

Reflection point

Can the emphasis on output within a technical organisation still adhere to the value base of an institutional organisation?

Figure 7.2: Health and social care institutional partnership model

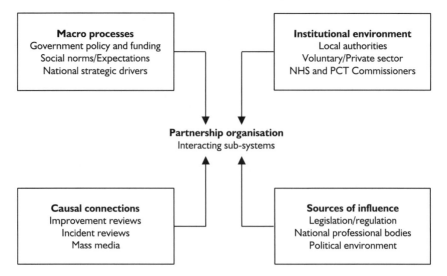

Macro processes
Government policy and funding
Social norms/Expectations
National strategic drivers

Institutional environment
Local authorities
Voluntary/Private sector
NHS and PCT Commissioners

Partnership organisation
Interacting sub-systems

Causal connections
Improvement reviews
Incident reviews
Mass media

Sources of influence
Legislation/regulation
National professional bodies
Political environment

The impact of foundation trusts

The drive within the NHS towards achieving foundation trust status, which has already been achieved by a number of mental health partnerships, is a key example of attempting to merge these aspects of organisational ethos. The Association of Directors of Social Services (ADSS) considered the move towards mental health foundation trusts in a 2007 paper by Watts, which concluded that there were both opportunities and risks to be considered within the new 'market' that foundation trusts would create. However, a significant concern remains that social care will not be properly represented, due to the weight of the health agenda and market forces.

> *there is a strong risk of social care interests not being effectively represented . . . The sheer weight of the health agenda is such that social care requires strong representation.*
> (Watts, 2007, p. 7)

If foundation trusts are able to ensure social care representation within their strategic direction and business planning processes, then the opportunities for competition and as a result high quality delivery of social care services, as well as a third type of organisation, which effectively spans the technical/institutional divide, may become a reality.

Facilitating partnership

For a partnership to be effective it requires support from both its internal sub-systems and its environmental influences. The level of influence that any one of these systems can exert has the potential to promote or sabotage the partnership.

There are a number of dimensions within the integration process, each of which needs to be considered and developed in order to deliver the proposed organisational partnership (Kagan and Neville, 1993).

(i) Service delivery

What is to be delivered and how will the organisation meet the requirements placed upon each of the partners? For mental health trusts this includes a range of community and inpatient services, which are governed by two sets of different regulations and legislation.

(ii) Programme linkage

The care programme approach defines this linkage within mental health services, and there is thus little scope for segregation that may affect other sectors. In reality, however, the full ideal of the seamless move between different mental health services has yet to be achieved.

(iii) Policy management

Many of the policies and procedures within mental health are multi-agency or based upon national guidelines. This creates a situation in which partners must cooperate and negotiate in order to meet the requirements placed upon them. Issues such as bed management policies and section 117 of the Mental Health Act 1983 require collaborative approaches to be applied.

(iv) Organisational structure

Representation of the social care perspective within partnership trusts remains an issue to be resolved. For many organisations, while they may have key strategic and leadership posts within the hierarchical structure, representation throughout the different levels of the organisation is variable. One of the main causes of this is what has been termed a 'take-over' by the NHS of mental health social care, whereby social care staff, and hence the social care approach, are often in the minority within large partnership organisations.

Consideration of each of these areas, and the identification of shared goals between partners, will facilitate the arrangements, and while this does not guarantee success it does increase its likelihood.

Barriers to partnership

Partnerships are complex entities and while varying elements can facilitate the process, these can also create barriers to the fruition of effective arrangements. Such barriers can be categorised into three distinct areas (Hodges et al., 1998):

- personal: people are key to partnership within organisations, and vested interests and power differentials can be significant hurdles to overcome;

- structural: incompatibility in data systems and inconsistent terms and conditions of employment are two key areas that create barriers within mental health services;

- environmental: the wider political agenda is a significant issue, as well as the pressures created by star ratings and performance measures.

These barriers were also considered in a paper published by the Social Care Institute for Excellence in 2005. This explored the possibilities of future integration across all adult services, and the experiences of mental health care were considered.

Among the barriers identified to improve joint working, the most substantial was the fundamental difference between universal and means-tested services. In addition, the health sector was considered insufficiently interested in social care because performance measures are not aligned. (Wistow, 2005, p. 4)

The issue of disparities between delivery of health care and social care services will be considered in depth in Chapter 8, in terms of the application of budgetary arrangements; however, it is also relevant to this debate as it is a fundamental issue that needs to be resolved.

Reflection points

What are the ethical considerations associated with providing some care packages free and requiring user contributions for others, within the same service?

What is the potential impact upon the staff delivering these services?

The impact of performance measurements

The regulatory bodies in health and social care provision are currently separate entities. Social care is regulated by the Commission for Social Care Inspection (CSCI), and health care by the Healthcare Commission (HCC). While on occasion these two bodies collaborate to undertake specific pieces of research or service reviews, the inspection and performance frameworks by which services are measured are not yet integrated. There are plans to merge the two regulatory bodies, and to put in place revised and converged standards by 2009, but until then partnership trusts are required to focus on and evidence two separate sets of performance measures.

This situation is causing some difficulties within organisations: for many trusts the social care standards and measures are a new requirement and they are unfamiliar. Matters such as data systems and evidence collation are still significant issues, and many services are required to double data entry in order to meet both set of requirements. This situation has an impact upon the organisational structure and management systems, as workers are unsure where their accountabilities and responsibilities lie, and are often resentful of what is viewed as ever-increasing bureaucracy.

This is not to suggest that regulatory standards are not essential – they provide both a framework for service delivery and a benchmark for best practice that should be central to provision. The issue here is that the different range of demands is directly affecting partnership effectiveness and hence the quality of provision. Currently each partner has its particular set of standards as the priority agenda, and it is difficult to negotiate priorities in a way which promotes the effectiveness of the whole system and which will be of tangible benefit to those who access the services provided

So far this discussion has focused upon application of a theoretical understanding of partnerships, and how these translate into practice environments. It is useful to have awareness and insight into the underpinning ideals when considering service development; however, this is not the full story. As part of this discussion it is necessary to consider how to measure whether a partnership is a success, and to explore the question of whether section 31 agreements are enabling organisations to make such judgements in an informed manner.

Measurement of success and failure in partnership arrangements

It is possible to review the written partnership agreements from a range of areas and authorities, because they are public documents and can be easily accessed. However, the reading of them is not quite so straightforward. Different areas have approached the collaborative delivery of mental health care differently, and the agreements reflect this inconsistency.

Some areas have included clear goals and performance measures from the outset; others have yet to establish that level of clarity, and it is therefore not possible to provide a definitive account of what is a success and what is a failure.

CSCI performance measures or successful application of the Health Care Commission core standards are an arbitrary measurement which is quantitative and does not evaluate the extent of partnership but rather how many people are served by each service. This is insufficient to draw conclusions regarding how well the partnership itself is performing.

Figure 7.3 makes some suggestions regarding how to measure success and failure. It is not a definitive list but rather an encouragement to consider and define successful outcomes of partnerships beyond what is measured by national regulatory frameworks and statistics.

For practitioners these concepts are not new and can equally be applied to the partnership between service user and worker – the principles are the same. For a partnership to work it requires the engagement and commitment of all parties, without which potential conflicts are created which can then become barriers rather than facilitators, both within the process and to the eventual outcome.

Overall, it is possible to suggest that due to the variations in the section 31 agreements that govern partnerships, it is often not possible to measure effectiveness in a meaningful way beyond that of the performance assessment frameworks that often correlate more closely to data quality than service quality. Without the development of clear and agreed

Figure 7.3: Characteristics of success and failure in partnership arrangements

Success	Failure
Shared goals	Conflicting agendas
Realistic timescales	Expecting immediate change
Leadership	Lack of direction and focus
Commitment	Indifference and lack of clarity
Shared vision	Unequal power balance
Collaborative decision-making	Blame culture
Effective communication	Hidden agendas
Collaboration and compromise	Manipulation/Domination
Proactive	Reactive

goals, evaluative processes and accountabilities, many partnerships have found themselves operating on a foundation of 'shifting sand' that is difficult to quantify, let alone qualify.

The final part of this chapter aims to translate the theoretical and organisational discussions thus far presented, into the practice environment. Beneath the various agreements, negotiations and political manoeuvrings, there is a group of professionals trying to provide 'safe, sound and supportive' services to individuals and communities affected by mental health problems and these need to be recognised and promoted.

Partnerships on a team and service level

For many professionals joint working with other disciplines has been one of their key functions, and for social work this is especially the case. The social work values of cooperation and collaboration with service users, carers, agencies and professionals in order to provide a holistic needs-led service pre-dates the political drivers by many years. The concepts of partnership working within this context are neither new nor innovative; the method of delivery is different but the principles have not changed. Despite this there have still been some struggles along the way, and social care workers have found themselves within NHS organisations feeling isolated and unsupported, anxious about what the new arrangements will mean to their professional careers and approaches. This is a human phenomenon: people do not usually adapt well to rapid change and the unfamiliar is often viewed with suspicion and defensive positioning (as discussed in Chapters 3 and 4).

The experience of workers across the sector is as varied as the organisational approaches. Some teams have taken easily to the arrangements, and embraced the opportunities that multi-professional working can bring; others have become like battle grounds, with each discipline drawing its metaphorical line in the sand that no other may cross.

The following case examples are taken from anecdotal accounts from practitioners working across the country. The different contexts at team level are not always dependent upon the wider organisational culture and need to be considered when exploring the elements that contribute to effective partnership working.

The team in Figure 7.4 has a shared goal of collaboration that each partner engages with, and the service delivered is inter-professional and open to evaluation from a range of perspectives – a context which facilitates learning and growth both within the team and within the individual practitioners. The organisational environment may have contributed to sustaining this arrangement but the working practices were in place prior to the application of the Health Act 1999 flexibilities and are thus not dependent upon strategic alliances and agendas.

While some service users accessing the team in Figure 7.5 receive high quality services, this is dependent upon the allocated care coordinator rather than the formation of practices across the team as a whole. As a result, disparities in provision are evident which reflect the wider system, as partnerships on a strategic level are also fragmented and in their infancy. This team's partnership success is more dependent upon the wider partnership arrangements as they were the catalyst for collaboration and there is little in the way of a shared team identity or ownership of the process.

Figure 7.4: Case study example – Northern Region Integrated Mental Health Team

Context

The team consists of representation from all disciplines, including the consultant psychiatrist, and secondments from voluntary sector organisations. Assessments are carried out by two professionals dependent upon capacity and taken back to the team for allocation to the most appropriate workers depending on individual needs. Decisions are made in weekly multi-disciplinary case conferences and input from all disciplines is available.

Outcome

Team members have a shared identity, feel supported and are valued as professionals; this facilitates collaboration and partnership, and improves service delivery.

Figure 7.5: Case study example – East Midlands Region CMHT

Context

The team was created by merging two community teams, one of which had social care professionals as well as health staff, and one which was solely comprised of community psychiatric nurses and a medical practitioner. The wider partnership arrangements came into force at the same time the team was formed. Social workers and nurses have separate offices within one building, and the psychiatric input is provided via the local acute unit. Team meetings occur once a week and case allocation is based upon capacity alone. If another discipline's input is required an official referral needs to be made.

Outcome

Team members are preoccupied by caseload levels and are supported by their own discipline; other alliances are based upon personal relationships rather than professional practices.

The team in Figure 7.6 is an example of where partnership is not being applied. While there are partnership agreements in existence across the whole service this area has created a co-existence rather than collaboration as each tries to preserve its own element of provision. This is not a sustainable position and the team in question is now being dissolved and restructured; however, they are not in isolation and professions and services across the country have faced a level of passive resistance at ground level. Without significant invest-ment in change management this situation will sabotage and create barriers to the ideal of joined-up, seamless partnership services.

Many other examples of how the integration of services has translated into front line service delivery could have been included; the variation of the experience is reflected on both a macro and micro level throughout the system, and there are no clear indicators to conclude whether partnership is becoming a reality on a national scale.

Figure 7.6: Case study example – South East Addictions Team

Context

There are two distinct teams and a range of specialists within this service. The social workers and nurses are in two separate teams with separate team management, different remits and different working conditions. The psychiatric and psychological input is provided by specialists who are based within the same service but have no shared accountability. A management group has been formed including the specialist practitioners and the team managers from each discipline. There is referral between the disciplines but no joint working and little collaboration on cases.

Outcome

The teams coexist but are not in partnership, and while the management group ensures representation of each discipline there is no shared agenda or goal. Practitioners require written referrals from each other and service users may be passed between waiting lists when demand is high. Defensive practice and stringent adherence to service area remits is evident.

Reflection point

Are your local services coexisting, conflicting or collaborating?

What evidence supports your view?

Is working in partnership possible between health and social care?

This chapter opened with a quote from Winston Churchill stating that together anything is possible; apart, failure is the most likely outcome. How far is this position applicable to the delivery and development of mental health services?

Theoretical approaches have been considered and applied to health and social care partnerships with some success. It is clear that a systems approach is appropriate in considering the formation and operation of partnership trusts; however, there is a range of barriers and facilitators that affects different partnerships to a greater or lesser extent. Regulation, interpretation and team formation have all had a significant impact on the integration of services.

There is no definitive answer as to whether partnership has been achieved, but it is possible to state that with the right context, environmental influences and organisational cultures the integration of services is possible. Further work is required in order to align legislative and statutory frameworks to ease and encourage the process.

Partnership is not defined solely by the location and mode of delivery of any given service, but rather is a culture and systems-wide approach that allows collaboration from the front line of delivery through to performance management and strategic planning. From the evidence and literature available in this area it appears that a significant amount of work and change are required before mental health services can be considered to be fully integrated health and social care partnerships.

Further reading

Hodges, S., Nesman, T. and Hernandez, M. (1998) *Promising Practices: Building Collaboration in Systems of Care*. Systems of Care Promising Practices in Mental Health Series, vol. 6. Washington, DC: American Institutes for Research.

Katz, D. and Kahn, R. L. (1978) *The Social Psychology of Organizations*. New York: John Wiley.

Wistow, G. (2005) *Developing Social Care: Past, Present, and Future*. SCIE: London.

Chapter 8

Health and social care budgets: will the fog ever lift?

Don't tell me where your priorities are. Show me where you spend your money and I'll tell you what they are. (James W. Frick, 1924–, US academic; *Think Exist Quotations*)

PQ framework

Achieving Post-qualifying Social Work awards

This chapter will assist in the meeting of National Occupational Standards for Social Work

Key Role 1, Unit 3: Assess needs and options to recommend a course of action.
Key Role 4, Unit 12: Assess and manage risk to individuals, families, carers, groups and communities.

For registered social workers considering, or working towards, post-qualifying awards, this chapter will also assist in meeting the requirements of both the specialist award in mental health, and the national occupational standards in mental health, which are core to the post-qualification standards in this area.

MHNOS 20: Work with individuals with mental health needs to negotiate and agree plans for addressing those needs.
MHNOS 56: Prioritise mental health interventions against available resources and the needs of the population.

PQ Specialist Award in Mental Health

47 (i) Recognising and managing creatively scarce resources and maximising there use.
47 (viii) Working in a person-centred way with complex individual and family situations.

Introduction

As this book has already discussed, the two areas of health and social care provision are becoming more and more interlinked. There is an emphasis on integrated services and 'seamless' provision that is user-led, but when it comes to the funding of care packages there are still many issues that result in a less than satisfactory outcome for many.

The government agenda has long been focused on 'joining up' provisions, with the modernisation agenda and a range of national service frameworks in both health and social care. More recently the government white paper *Our Health, Our Care, Our Say* (DoH, 2006) made significant progress by creating a joint agenda for service improvement which spans both provision and commissioning. It placed the strategic direction into the realms of integrated community services designed around those it served. Yet despite these initiatives there remain many unresolved issues, and the separation of health needs and social needs in terms of funding criteria creates a conflict within the overall policy direction (Bradshaw, 2002).

The contrast between integration on the one hand and separation on the other has given rise to a particular paradox. And while professional practice and community-based provision are becoming more aligned with identification of core skills and interventions, the purchasing and commissioning of external services to support these activities are becoming more fragmented.

The emphasis here is upon the rules and operation of two distinct funding and eligibility frameworks that exist within the context of integrated service provision. The health and social care funding processes are among the last battalions of separate provision, although the application process in itself is applied by the same group of staff. The question that now needs to be addressed is whether it is time that pragmatism was applied to this area in order to ensure that service users receive the best possible services to meet their needs.

The aim of this chapter is to consider the budgetary arrangements in place for purchasing and procurement of services, and consider the issue of funding care packages from within an otherwise integrated service delivery framework.

Funding packages of care

The continuing health and social care funding criteria and application processes are administered within different agencies and against different priorities; however, the boundaries between the two are far from clear. In the case of continuing care funding, this is held within the primary care trusts (PCTs) which are largely commissioning bodies, for social care decision making is held within local authorities (LAs), which are both commissioners and partners within the overall provision.

Applications are generally made by both health and social care staff within NHS Trusts and LAs, with acceptance (or rejection) based on the evidence from needs assessments carried out by these staff.

In June 2007 a national framework for continuing health care was published, the aim of which was to clarify the operation of the funding criteria. This was implemented in October 2007 and has, to a certain extent, simplified the process. However, there remains a high degree of subjectivity in the application of the criteria which is yet to be resolved. Mental health service users in particular are subject to debate in this area, as in many cases the distinction between what is a primary health need and what is a primary social care need are less the satisfactorily defined.

The problem of definition

It is difficult to define what is health and what is social care: the difference between the two areas has historically been a key issue in both service provision and multi-disciplinary discussion. The following definitions are included in order to clarify the scope of what may be included within each term.

Health
The state of complete physical, mental and social well-being. (WHO, 1998)

Health care
Any type of services provided by professionals or paraprofessionals with an impact on health status. (WHO, 1998)

Social care
The term 'social care' covers a wide range of services, which are provided by local authorities and the independent sector. Social care comes in many forms, such as care at home, in day centres or by way of residential or nursing homes. The term also covers services such as providing meals on wheels to the elderly, home help for people with disabilities and fostering services. (DoH, 2006)

These definitions are far from adequate, and do not indicate what needs are contained within each. The subjective nature of assessment, which is based not only on a professional's level of skill but also on the perspective and personal bias that they bring to the task, is not resolved by these definitions. Maximising the service user's level of biopsychosocial functioning and assessing the risk are the key areas evidenced when any application for funding is made, but whether this is a health need or a social care need is often very difficult to determine.

Health and social care: integration or exclusion?

There have been a number of recent debates about care funding. Commentators from the social care sector, in particular, are vocal on the subject. For example, Jeff Jerome, co-chair of the Association of Directors of Social Services Disabilities Committee, has commented:

We are still concerned that it will leave local authorities with a moral obligation to fund people who we are not legally supposed to support.
(Cited in *Community Care Magazine*, 22 March 2007)

The mental health service user group in particular faces difficulties in accessing funding, as a result of the complex and varied nature of their presenting needs. There are many instances reported (for example by the BBC, Alzheimer's Society, Age Concern, Independent Age and the Disability Alliance), that detail cases where individuals with high levels of care needs are not being given access to the help they need, or who are being required to pay for their own care. These appear to be mainly due to disputes between primary care trusts (PCTs) and LAs as to whether the primary need is based in health or social care.

Reflection point

How do you define a health need or a social care need within your practice?

Application of funding criteria

Both continuing care and social care funding mechanisms have stated criteria, which relate to the need that an individual is presenting with. In the case of continuing care a number of areas are considered when making an assessment: these are the nature, complexity, intensity and unpredictability of needs within the 12 care domains, which are as follows (DoH, 2007b):

> *Behaviour; Cognition; Communication; Mobility; Nutrition – Food and Drink; Continence; Skin (including tissue viability); Breathing; Drug Therapies and Medication: Symptom Control; Psychological Needs; Altered States of Consciousness.*

In each instance the individual's needs within the care domains is rated according to a severity scale; in order to be eligible for 100 per cent NHS continuing care funding the individual must have an assessed need that meets at least one of the following three criteria:

1. High Level Dependency – defined as where the withdrawal or non-availability of intensive and/or frequent healthcare would threaten survival, or where they have a need for clinical input from a doctor, nurse, therapist, or other member of the multi-disciplinary team regularly, because of the instability and/or complexity and/or intensity and/or unpredictability of their medical condition.

2. Highly Challenging Behaviour – people falling under this criterion will be at high risk of harm to themselves and/or to others, and have an established history of, or potential for, severe behavioural problems requiring clinical input from a doctor, nurse, therapist or other member of the multi disciplinary team regularly because of the instability and/or complexity and/or intensity and/or unpredictability of their medical condition.

3. End Stage Terminal Illness – a progressive state of decline, for example, with a life expectancy of less than three months. (Bedfordshire and Hertfordshire Strategic Health Authority, 2003; pp. 9–11)

The National Service Framework for continuing care states that the question of whether the primary need is a health need looks 'at the totality of the relevant needs' (DoH, 2007b) and addresses the following questions:

- Taken as a whole, are the nursing or other health services required by the individual more than incidental or ancillary to the provision of accommodation which Local Authority Social Services are under a duty to provide; and

- Are they of a nature beyond which a Local Authority, whose primary responsibility is to provide Social Services, could be expected to provide?

(DoH, 2006, pp. 7–8)

It appears from these statements that continuing care funding is granted on the premise that the care required is above and beyond what would be provided by the LA under social care funding guidelines. This premise is one that creates difficulties in the assessment decision, largely as a result of the complex and wide-ranging definition of what constitutes social care.

Fair access to care – social care funding frameworks

The rules governing social care are based upon the *Fair Access to Care* policy documentation, which sets out an eligibility framework for local authority funding decisions. The interpretation of the eligibility bandings is subject to local interpretation: for example, the understanding of the term 'vital' can involve a number of issues and is subject to social change. In previous years, social services departments provided assistance with bathing, but over the past five years the view of this has changed. It is now not considered to be a vital need, and instead personal care support concentrates on washing rather than assisting an individual to bathe.

Figure 8.1 sets out the top bandings of this criterion in detail. Many LAs, in light of dwindling resources, have drawn a metaphorical line in the sand and stated that funding will be

Figure 8.1: Fair access to care eligibility criteria (DoH, 2003, p. 4)

Critical	Substantial
• Life is, or will be, threatened; and/or	• There is, or will be, only partial choice and control over the immediate environment; and/or
• Significant health problems have developed or will develop; and/or	
• There is, or will be, little or no choice and control over vital aspects of the immediate environment; and/or	• Abuse or neglect has occurred or will occur; and/or
	• There is, or will be, an inability to carry out the majority of personal care or domestic routines; and/or
• Serious abuse or neglect has occurred or will occur; and/or	
• There is, or will be, an inability to carry out vital personal care or domestic routines; and/or	• Involvement in many aspects of work, education or learning cannot or will not be sustained; and/or
• Vital involvement in work, education or learning cannot or will not be sustained; and/or	• The majority of social support systems and relationships cannot or will not be sustained; and/or
• Vital social support systems and relationships cannot or will not be sustained; and/or	• The majority of family and other social roles and responsibilities cannot or will not be undertaken.
• Vital family and other social roles and responsibilities cannot or will not be undertaken.	

granted to those presenting with substantial or above levels of need. The difficulty that has arisen is that the thresholds for social care are very similar to those of continuing care, especially within the domains of behaviour, cognition, communication and psychological needs, and as a result both funding authorities are increasingly keen to pass the funding responsibility to the other to relieve budgetary pressures.

When considering both sets of eligibility criteria there is a lack of clarity concerning which is most appropriate, because in mental health terms is it based on subjectivity and levels of risk rather than a concrete and consistent assessment of how the condition affects the individual's level of functioning.

Risk assessment is not an exact science in any environment, and looks at the likelihood of harm occurring in light of previous and present circumstances, many of which are social considerations in themselves. In addition the skill applied by the assessor in arguing a case can also be a key consideration and indicator of whether funding will be agreed.

Risk – an inexact science

How an individual perceives risk is key within this discussion. Mental health professionals and commissioners are adept at saying the word but very often give no real indication of what they mean. Risk of harm is the area which creates the most anxiety among professionals, but this term usually refers to violence and self-harm/suicide. In reality the risks of relapse, neglect, social isolation or withdrawal have far more impact upon an individual's quality of life.

Positive risk-taking is also an often neglected activity in mental health care; it appears that the right to take risks is often played down by professionals in favour of a protection emphasis which, while valid, in some cases does not account for the individual's right to experience the whole of the human experience.

The case study in Figure 8.2 examines the two sets of criteria and demonstrates the complexity of defining which set of criteria are relevant to the range of needs presented.

Assessment considerations

For those individuals being assessed for both continuing care and social care funding, one consideration is that of their own personal finances. Those who are funded from social care budgets are required to undertake means testing and ultimately contribute to the cost of their care, whereas those who receive continuing care funding receive their services free at the point of access. This constitutes a significant impact upon individuals and their families, especially when the distinction between what is health and what is social care is so subjective.

As well as having subjectivity in distinction, there is also a disparity in the systems, which increases the already evident paradox within integrated health and social care. There exists a system of joined-up care, but the purchasing of additional services remains separated and there is a disparity between what is charged and what is not. If health and social care are

Figure 8.2: Case study example – Mr S

Mr S has recently been detained in an acute psychiatric institution under section 3 of the Mental Health Act 1983. On admission he was suffering from drug-induced psychosis, and had become increasingly subject to paranoid and delusional beliefs which included thinking that he was being followed and was going to be killed as part of a plot.

Mr S had been refusing to leave his home, had barricaded himself into his flat and had been stockpiling food and other household essentials. He stopped attending his work placement three months ago and refused to see any of his friends or family. The stockpiled food had been rotting in his flat as he had not been eating it, which had created a significant risk to his health. In addition he had not been sleeping, had a history of non-compliance with medication, and had been neglecting his personal care as he believed that if he turned the taps on his 'enemies' could get to him.

Mr S has been admitted on seven occasions during the last two years and his symptoms have been deteriorating and becoming more extreme with each admission. He had on this occasion started to harm himself by cutting, and had been verbally and physically aggressive when the assessing team had tried to access his flat.

At his last CPA review it was felt by his care team that Mr S needed more support that he had been receiving previously and the assessment showed that supported living and a significant care package were required. Mr S's needs are compatible with both continuing care and social care for the reasons shown below.

1. Assessment against continuing care criteria
Challenging behaviour – Severe
Aggression, harm to self, non compliance and resistance to care, severe fluctuations in mental state.

Psychological needs – High
Mood disturbance or anxiety symptoms or periods of distress that have a severe impact on the individual's health and/or well-being.

Withdrawn from any attempts to engage them in support, care planning and daily activities.

Drug therapy/medication regime – Severe
Risk of non-concordance with medication, placing them at severe risk of relapse.

Altered states of consciousness – High
ASC that require skilled intervention to reduce the risk of harm.

This assessment shows two incidences of severe needs and would therefore meet the criteria of continuing health care funding. However, this rating is subjective, and – 'the interactions between needs in different care domains, and the evidence from risk assessments, should be taken into account in deciding whether a recommendation of eligibility for NHS Continuing Healthcare should be made' (DoH, 2007b).

2. Assessment against social care criteria

Mr S's mental states, social engagement, engagement with care, self-care and risk to health all constitute a critical risk to his independence and therefore meet the social care funding requirements for critical banding due to the following factors:

- significant health problems have developed or will develop;
- there is, or will be, little or no choice and control over vital aspects of the immediate environment;
- vital social support systems and relationships cannot or will not be sustained;
- vital involvement in work, education or learning cannot or will not be sustained;
- there is, or will be, an inability to carry out vital personal care or domestic routines.

both essential needs when considering a person's independence and quality of life, how can it be fair to apply means testing to one area and not to the other?

The critical and substantial criteria of *Fair Access to Care* are very similar to those of priority, high and severe needs within continuing care. All these bands state that there is a high dependency need, and that without the provision of care there could be a critical impact upon the individual's life (either mortality or morbidity). As a result the question then becomes whether the cause of the need should determines whether or not the service user has to pay.

This type of debate is comparable the distinction made at the outset of the welfare state between the deserving and undeserving poor (Glasby, 2006), with those who were 'sick' being supported by the state, whereas those who were deemed 'needy' were not.

As already discussed throughout this text, the overall policy direction of central government is driving towards integrated care, with joint white papers, integrated multi-disciplinary teams, and a focus on skill mixes among professionals that is generic across the client group. With this being the case, is the gap between NHS funded and social care means-tested provisions possible to operate within an environment of integrated care and service provision, and where do we draw the line between health care and social care needs?

Reflection point

Can integration of services be successful while separate funding streams exist?

Health care or social care: is there a line to be drawn?

So how do we define, let alone determine, whether a need is one of health care or social care? There are many commentators on the issue (for example the Association of Directors of Social Services, the Royal College of Nursing, Age Concern, MIND, Disability Alliance, the Alzheimer's Society, and Mental Health Alliance), but it appears that these largely speak from one perspective or the other and it is therefore difficult to ascertain the balance between the two. The converse perspective between the medical and social models, as discussed in Chapter 4, also contributes to this debate. The lack of definition of mental health issues, and the difficulty in stating whether an individual's needs are as a direct result of the mental illness or due to wider social care considerations, compound the confusion when dealing with eligibility within this service user group, and the identification of specific needs is often less than clear.

A recent report by the Health Service Select Committee attempted to address the issue, but again there was little guidance as to where the line should be drawn They stated:

> *In examining the problems and issues surrounding NHS continuing care, we begin by considering the separation of health and social care systems, which necessitates a whole range of distinctions between personal, nursing and health care which are largely artificial and impossible to administer, and which, arguably, underpin all the current difficulties in funding continuing care.* (Health Service Select Committee, 2005, p. 10)

This statement does not help the process, though again it identifies the problem. Legal cases such as Grogan and Coughlan did this adequately; there is no further need to continue to make this definition, but rather to seek a solution. These cases are briefly outlined in Figure 8.3.

Figure 8.3: Continuing health care legal judgments

R v North and East Devon Health Authority ex p Coughlan
(Decided by the Court of Appeal in July 1999)
Ms Coughlan, a severely disabled resident living at a nursing home, was promised that it was a 'home for life'. Later the health authority believed the home had become uneconomic and proposed to close it and move Ms Coughlan elsewhere. The health authority believed that community care law changes had effectively transferred the provision of nursing care to social services departments from health authorities and that it was thus no longer empowered to provide or arrange general long-term nursing care. The health authority did not identify an alternative placement for Ms Coughlan before deciding to close the home, and there had been only been medical and nursing assessment of her needs.

The Court of Appeal ruled that the health authority had failed to meet its obligations, and had unlawfully applied eligibility criteria in this case. In addition it stated that the authority had breached Ms Coughlan's human rights under article 8: the right to respect for family and private life, by moving her from what she considered to be her home.

R on the application of Grogan v Bexley NHS Care Trust and others (2006)
(High court judgment on the assessment criteria used when determining eligibility for continuing health care)

The claimant was a 65-year-old lady who had multiple sclerosis, dependent oedema with the risk of ulcers breaking out, double incontinence and some cognitive impairment.

She had been assessed as not qualifying for NHS continuing health care but argued that the decision to deny her full NHS funding was unlawful, since the eligibility criteria put in place by South East London SHA (Strategic Health Authority) were contrary to the judgment in the Coughlan case.

Defining need

The definition of a 'need' is complex in itself, let alone whether the nature of the need is health- or social care-based. As already mentioned, the split between free and means-tested care provision is reminiscent of the 1940s legislation which led to the creation of the UK welfare state. The assumption that it is possible to distinguish between people who are sick and people who are frail and disabled is somewhat of a red herring. In Chapter 3 the nature of social care was highlighted as a socio-economic and political concept, which varied according to government policy and priorities. With this being the case the attempt to define such care appears somewhat academic.

It is possible to have the same debate regarding what constitutes a need. In sociological terms the need is relative, and defined in comparison to the social norms and culture within which the individual operates. While there are a number of basic needs, for example nutrition and hydration, many of the other needs that are commonly identified within community care services are subject to the expectations of society. For example, engagement in meaningful activity is now seen as a key need; however, 20 years ago this was not a consideration as maintenance was the emphasis rather than well-being.

The nature and cause of an individual's needs are often attributed to either a health or a social care factor, but in reality there is rarely this distinction. The discussion in Chapter 4 concerning the medical and social models of mental distress emphasised that a holistic consideration of individuals' circumstances is required if their well-being and recovery are to be supported; however, while the evidence base and policy direction on the whole support this view, the funding framework does not.

It is stated by many commentators that the nature of any given need is also defined by the subjectivity of the assessor (Parry-Jones and Soulsby, 2001; Lightfoot, 1995; Dalley, 1991; Illich, 1977), and that it is therefore hardly surprising that there is confusion and conflict in this area. Mental health issues and needs can be both a primary health need and a primary social care need, and it is essentially within the realms of the level of skill of the assessor to argue the case to ensure that the service user's needs are met. The funding pressures that face both health and social service departments will continue to be a debated area and the requirements on the assessors to provide detailed analysis and evidence will remain paramount.

Reflection point

How do you define the term 'need' within your practice?

Practicalities of providing for care needs

There are many examples of service users whose needs are left unmet while continuing care and social care panels debate who is responsible for meeting the presenting needs. There appears to be a tendency for reactionary, rather than proactive, interventions from both policy and operational perspectives. High profile media cases and legal challenges are two such areas that have an impact upon policy formulation. For example, the Grogan and Coughlan cases led to the review of the continuing care framework, but while the eligibility rules were clarified as a result of these cases, the policy does not assist in closing the gap between defining the terms health and social care needs, as this was not the emphasis in this instance. This type of policy making is often not sufficient, and further challenges will be raised which will ultimately lead to further revisions, rather than looking at the whole system in an attempt to define clear definitions and pathways.

The following case studies (Figure 8.4 and 8.5) are examples drawn from practice examples. These cases demonstrate that despite the raft of legal challenges, and government attempts to address the frameworks for continuing care and social care needs, there are still many conflicts which lead to a deficiency in service provision.

It is clear that the subjectivity of funding decisions and the inter-professional wrangling between LAs and PCTs can be problematic. The case of Mr X is a classic one within mental health services. There are obviously arguments on both sides which are valid, but while this argument continues Mr X is being detained and his liberty and care needs are not being properly met.

Figure 8.4: Case study example – Mr X

Mr. X is a 52-year-old white British male, diagnosed with personality disorder, bipolar disorder and alcohol dependence. He has a history of inpatient admissions, homelessness and challenging behaviour.

Mr X was placed on section 3 of the Mental Health Act 1983 in December 2005 and detained to a local acute mental health unit. Since admission his mental health has been stabilised; however his long-term needs suggest that a residential specialist placement is now required. Mr X was referred to a specialist resource and accepted for placement in June 2006. A funding application was placed for social care funding. At the funding panel an assessment under continuing care criteria was requested, as it was felt that there were health care needs that superseded his social care needs.

Mr X was subsequently re-assessed under continuing health care criteria, and it was agreed that his health care needs were the predominate issue in his case. This assessment went to the continuing care panel in July 2006. The panel disputed the assessment and said it was a social care issue. In the meantime Mr X's health deteriorated: unsteady gait and urinary incontinence were added to his difficulties. As a result, on its return to the social care funding panel, the panel said it was a health issue; the continuing care panel continued to disagree.

Mr X was then re-assessed under both fair access to care and continuing care criteria. It was determined that he met both sets of criteria, but neither panel would accept responsibility for funding the specialist placement required.

Resulting situation

In February 2007, Mr X was still in hospital under section 3 of the Mental Health Act 1983. His mental health was stable, but there was now some evidence of depression, due largely to continued inpatient detention which was wholly inappropriate to his needs. The care team felt unable to remove the section 3, as Mr X wanted to leave the unit, and his health and safety and the nature of his condition were such as to raise fears that he would be at very significant risk if discharged. The panels were still in disagreement over whose responsibility it was to fund his care and so his placement was still not able to be agreed.

Reflection point

The nature of mental health needs is highly contested: is it health or is it social care?

In reality, Mr X's needs are both health and social, and in cases such as this a compromise needs to be reached or responsibility taken by one of the authorities. In the context of budgetary and resource restraints this is often the last option for the parties involved to consider.

Figure 8.5: Case study example – Mrs Y

Mrs Y is an 80-year-old white British female. She is married, and living at home with her husband. Mrs Y suffers from severe dementia, and there is also evidence of auditory and visual hallucination. She presents a range of challenging behaviour, including violence towards her husband (carer). Mrs Y was assessed by social services who recommended that high level nursing care was needed to meet her needs. Continuing care was contacted, but an assessment was refused due to social care involvement. There has been no hospital admission as the responsible medical officer stated that inpatient admission is inappropriate.

Mrs Y's risk at home is very high, and her husband is under extreme stress. Social care has agreed to fund a placement, but at a rate of £589 per week. The only home able to offer accommodation at this price that is appropriate for her presenting needs is 200 miles away. Mrs Y's husband is willing to travel if necessary but will incur expense as there is no service that is willing to reimburse him, and he cannot afford the additional cost. Mrs Y's care manager feels this distance is inappropriate, but social care will not increase the funding ceiling as it is due to a health care need that a specialist placement is required. The continuing care service states that social care services need to meet the additional costs, and they are unable to assess due to current social care involvement and a prior funding agreement which must mean that the need is predominantly a social care one.

> **Resulting situation**
> Mrs Y is a very vulnerable lady: she is disorientated, confused and presenting with critical needs and risks, but is being left at home with her husband who is unable to cope and meet her needs appropriately. This appears to be mainly due to disagreements in regard to whose responsibility it is to fund a specialist placement.

Again it appears that Mrs Y's needs could be considered under both health and social care frameworks; however, as is often the case, neither is willing to allocate its budgets when it could be argued and passed to the other. It appears that panels applying the same criteria can reach very different conclusions on the same cases (Vindlacheruvu and Luxton, 2006), due to the subjective nature of what a need is, as Dinsdale stated in 2006:

> The lack of uniformity in the eligibility criteria [around the country] has meant that access to funding is fragmented, and has resulted in many patients being wrongly denied funding. (Dinsdale, 2006, p. 7)

These case studies are not unusual – contact with integrated mental health and care management teams across the country would reveal more examples of the conflict that occurs between health and social care funding. The needs of those most vulnerable within our communities are not being met due to the debate over what a need actually is and what is its basis.

One final consideration within the field of mental health that merits discussion is that of section 117 of the Mental Health Act 1983. This is a provision for free aftercare for those who have been detained on a treatment section. It provides for a joint responsibility between health and social care agencies to meet the aftercare needs of the individual; however, there is no provision in funding guidelines for joint funding packages of care. Even when there is a clear joint duty to provide care, there thus remains a debate between the two agencies regarding whose responsibility it is to meet the cost.

Is there a solution?

It is clear from the practical situation, commentaries and legal challenges that the current situation of separation between health and social care funding is not tenable, at least not in a way that will meet the needs and care requirements of the service user population. The framework for continuing care which was fully implemented in October 2007 does provide some clarity, and the decision-making tools and regulations that accompany it assist in this process. However, the definitions of what constitutes a health need and what constitutes a social care need within the mental health service user group remains a difficult and subjective determination.

The legal challenges and high profile cases (which usually result in a judgment of system failure), although highlighting the issues of gaps in service, often do not resolve them. The policy making aimed at addressing these difficulties is inevitably developed within a political context, and remains dependent upon wider economic considerations. The recognition that subjectivity is often at the heart of funding decision needs to be owned and addressed if progress towards true user-led integrated service provision is to be achieved.

The impact of stigma

One further consideration that must be noted is that the mental health service user group is often stigmatised and marginalised within our society, and decision makers are as affected by cultural and social norms as any other group. While professionals must always strive to identify their own prejudices and how these impact upon their practice, this does not negate the fact that there is an impact. The social definition of need has already been discussed, but it is worth reiterating here as the service users in question are perhaps one of the most affected groups in terms of social exclusion and stereotyping within politics, the public and the media environments.

The continual debates between funding panels and professional groups is indicative of the confusion inherent in the policy and guidance within this area, and urgent action is therefore needed to reconcile these differences.

> *The scale of this problem is unbelievable . . . At present some older people, who are paying all the costs of their care, have higher needs than those who are fully funded in other areas. These figures indicate the ultimate post code lottery.*
> (Lishman, cited in Age Concern, 2007)

It seems that in all other areas of policy development the focus is on integrating care services, whether we are considering the partnership and pooled budgetary arrangements enabled under the Health Act 1999, or the joint white paper (DoH, 2006) which set out the vision for integrated and 'seamless' service provision across the health and social care divides. With this being the case, the question that remains is why funding for care services is still separated, especially given the problems of determining which category an individual's needs falls within.

Practice-based commissioning is another stream of funding that may become increasingly utilised. The 2006 white paper gave the primary health care sector the power to commission services directly (with the approval of the PCT) under the practice based commissioning (PBC) arrangements. Some examples of the application of this initiative include:

- South West Staffordshire: a group of GP practices has purchased a local residential home with support from the Alzheimer's Society, which means that residential, respite and day care services are all easily accessible to patients of the consortia of practices involved.

- Bexley: a consortia of GP practices has commissioned the Rapid Response Team to develop patient pathways with the local home care providers, ambulance teams and hospital clinical assessment services. The aim is to ensure that local people can receive appropriate adjustments to their home care and health care package in the community.

Schemes such as these are far more reflective of the integrated nature of modern health and social care provision, and go a significant way towards resolving the paradox that the traditional segregated funding criteria and panel applications create. The move towards localised service commissioning is still in its infancy and the take-up of this option is not yet widespread. There is, however, potential for this type of provision to take over from segregated health and social care funding streams, in order to establish a more holistic and needs-led commissioning strategy across the national stage.

> **Reflection point**
>
> What is the potential for PBC initiatives to influence care service delivery in your area?

The types of care provided under the two funding streams are often very similar in nature – for example, residential provision and home care packages – and thus it is not too far a leap to combine these provisions. This was the rationale in integrated service provision in the first instance. For example, while medical and social work professions come with a different perspective and different interventions, the aim of improving the quality of life for the service user is common to all: should this not also be the central premise of the funding debate?

Will the fog ever lift?

This chapter began with a quote from James W. Frick, who stated that the priorities can be defined by what money is spent upon. This rationale supports the socio-economic and political context which the health and social care debate inhabits. The current priority is well-being, and issues such as direct payments and self-managed care, which place the service user as the decision-maker and commissioner of their own care, are therefore receiving significant emphasis within the field. Despite this emphasis the social care and health care funding frameworks have yet to catch up with developments, and it appears that the definition of the cause of any given need is far more debated than the need itself. This could be seen as a reflection of the whole health and social care paradox, which is continuing to be fuelled by competing political and financial agendas that affect the sector.

As discussed, issues such as full integration of the funding streams and services, the development of a clear definition of a health or social care need, and utilisation of initiatives such as practice based commissioning and individual budgets may all assist in resolving the dilemmas. There is no easy answer, but the one clear message that can be drawn from this discussion is that the current system of separation and segregation is not working in practice. Within a environment of integrated services surely there is a way to bring together continuing care and social care in a way which meets the needs of all involved.

Further reading

Department of Health (2003) *Fair Access to Care Services: Guidance on Eligibility Criteria*. London: TSO.

Department of Health (2007b) *National Framework for NHS Continuing Health Care and NHS Funded Care in England*. London: TSO.

Chapter 9

Integrated services: where do the service users fit in?

The benefit for clients is that they have a single care plan, a single key or link worker and a united multi-disciplinary team to deal with whatever health or social care need they have. (DoH, 2000, p. 71)

PQ framework

Achieving Post-qualifying Social Work awards

This chapter will assist in the meeting of National Occupational Standards for Social Work:

Key Role 6, Unit 18:   Research, analyse and evaluate current knowledge of best practice in social work.

Key Role 1, Unit 3:   Assess needs and options to recommend a course of action

For registered social workers considering, or working towards, post-qualifying awards, this chapter will also assist in meeting the requirements of both the specialist award in mental health and the national occupational standards in mental health, which are core to the post-qualification standards in this area.

MHNOS 19:   Coordinate, monitor, and review service responses to meet individual needs and circumstances.

MHNOS 57:   Monitor, evaluate and improve processes for delivering mental health services to a population.

PQ Specialist Award in Mental Health

47 (vi)   Working proactively to provide care that makes a positive difference.

47 (x)   Utilising knowledge and research from people who use services.

Introduction

The central premise of integrating health and social care services is that the quality of patient experience, and the ability of providers to meet local needs, will be enhanced. Traditionally, users of mental health services have had to negotiate a complex system of health and social care providers, with little in terms of communication and collaboration between them. This was recognised in the late 1990s as an area that needed development and the integration of care was encouraged across all care providers.

Somerset Partnership Trust was one of the first organisations to combine social care and health within one remit, via a partnership arrangement. This arrangement, between Somerset County Council and Somerset Health Authority, enabled the transfer, via secondment, of social care staff to an NHS organisation, and the delegation of a range of social services functions to the trust. A number of other partnerships were created in the next five years, with Lincolnshire, Sandwell, Camden and Islington, Hertfordshire and Bedfordshire and Luton all forming Mental Health and Social Care Partnership NHS Trusts, responsible for the delivery of the full range of health and social care services for mental health care in their respective areas.

So far this book has explored a range of issues associated with the integration of health and social care services from the perspective of the professionals involved and with a focus upon the policy focus. It appears that the experience and effectiveness of integrated mental health services are variable across the country, and although there is more of a consensus in terms of the philosophy of quality and improvement, there is still disagreement over how this translates into practice.

The aim of this chapter is to explore the issues from the perspective of those who need and use the services. The central focus of integrating health and social care is to join up provision and so improve the patient journey. This chapter explores whether the ideal and the reality of integrated services are consistent, and asks the questions – what does integration mean to those who use the services, and does it improve the quality of the care provided?

Service user feedback – what is important in service provision?

Since 2003, the NHS has conducted an annual survey across mental health provisions, both among the staff and also among the individuals who access the services they provide. The aim of these surveys is to collate a cross-section of feedback from service users on which to base service improvement strategies.

Nationally, the response rate is encouraging and provides a sample from which the effectiveness of service provision can be rated. In addition, in 2005/6 the Health Care Commission (HCC) and the Commission for Social Care Inspection (CSCI) carried out a joint review of mental health services which encompassed approximately 7,500 individuals using community mental health services across the country. A number of key factors were identified as a result of this review as being vital to effective service delivery – Figure 9.1 outlines these areas.

These elements also represent the key themes of policy direction and are consistent with drivers such as the 2006 joint health and social care white paper; they formed the basis of the joint review in terms of an assessment framework. The issue of partnership working, although stated as being among the vital elements, was not considered as an overall issue

Figure 9.1: Vital elements of effective services

1. Access to services
2. A 'whole person' or holistic approach
3. To address social exclusion
4. To ensure that people who use services are empowered to be involved in their own care
5. To enable carers to be properly involved in the care of those using the services
6. To empower people who use services, and their families, to fully engage in the planning of services
7. For organisations to work in partnership.

(From HCC and CSCI, 2007, p. 13)

Figure 9.2: Secondment arrangements – rating of care services received as good or better (per cent), 2004–7

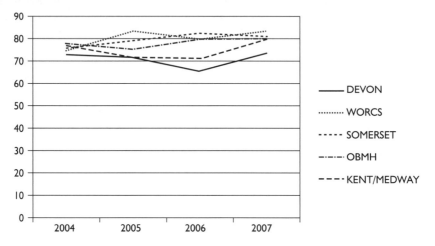

within the joint review; however, specific areas such as availability of crisis services and the care coordinator role were examined.

There is little in the literature, or the inspection standards applied to the field, which gives a definitive answer in terms of whether the joining up of health and social care services has made any real difference to the service user population, and the data from patients' surveys, reviews and anecdotal evidence will therefore be analysed in order to draw conclusions as to whether mental health services on the ground have improved since the joining up of provision.

Patient surveys – what are the lessons?

The starting point in the annual surveys is how the services are rated overall. Chapters 5 and 6 considered the different models of integrated services and the results of the service user feedback will be considered using the same distinctions. Figures 9.2 and 9.3 illustrate the rating of several mental health trusts, which have chosen either secondment or full integration of provision as their mode of operation. The results span 2004–7, a period when all the trusts illustrated undertook organisational change in order to 'join up' the services they provide.

Figure 9.2 suggests that the authorities that have entered into secondment arrangements have had some variability in terms of their ratings among users of the service, with Devon demonstrating the widest range of between 71 and 80 per cent approval ratings. All but one authority (Worcester) experienced a drop in their ratings during the change process. For example, in 2006 Kent and Medway underwent a period of organisational change into the new trust format, and at this time their rating fell to 66 per cent; this trend is reflected elsewhere with a drop to 76 per cent for Oxfordshire and Buckinghamshire Trust during their change phase. Despite this trend, all of the seconded trust arrangements have seen an increase in their approval ratings between 2006 and 2007.

Those trusts that opted for full integration of services appear to have followed a slightly different path from those that entered into secondment arrangements in terms of their approval ratings among service users. From the trusts selected, the majority have seen a steady increase in their ratings, the notable exception being Sandwell which has fluctuated across the period. The correlation between organisational change and service user approval is not as evident as it was with the secondment arrangements, with only Bedfordshire and Luton following this pattern. This may be as a result of change occuring at an earlier point, with most trusts undertaking their integrative arrangements prior to the commencement of the patient surveys within mental health.

Social care performance ratings

Social care performance assessment is currently based on service delivery rather than the patient view; although a new inspection framework which is more outcome-focused was introduced in 2007, the data available is still currently related to process rather than outcome.

Figure 9.3: Full Integration – rating of care services received as good or better, 2004–7 (per cent)

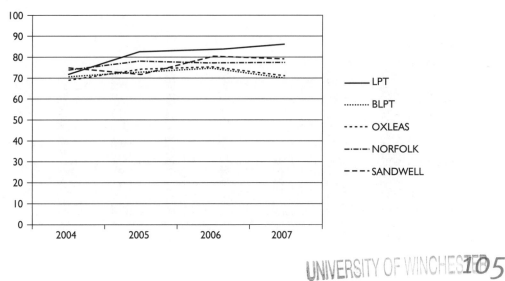

Figure 9.4 illustrates authority ratings in terms of the key indicator of 'help to live at home for mental health service users' across the time span of 2000–06.

The trusts with the widest variation of rating – Devon and Sandwell – do illustrate a correlation with the period of organisational change. Devon integrated in 2001 and the following review (2003/4) saw a significant drop; Sandwell undertook its change in 2005, the year in which it jumped two points in terms of its rating.

The data so far considered suggests that while organisational alignment does have an impact upon the ability to provide quality services, this is more closely related to the undertaking of the change itself rather than the improvement of services as a result.

This must be considered in light of the limited amount of data available specifically considering this point, and also in view of the short time since some trusts completed their integration. This view has previously been supported in the 2004 Social Services Inspectorate paper *Treated as People*, which stated (p. 2):

> *Organisational change is a necessary part of the reform of mental health services. But it can easily dominate activity and dilute good services.*

At this point the information is still far from conclusive, and further evidence needs to be considered in order to draw balanced conclusions.

Coordinated care

The Department of Health issued a paper in 2002 entitled *Positive Approaches to the Integration of Health and Social Care in Mental Health Services*, which stated that integrated services place service users and carers at the 'heart' of the provision as they allow service models to consider context, as well as diagnosis, in a coordinated manner. The emphasis on joining up health care and social care is stated to be the preference of the service user (DoH, 2002), as it facilitates easier and less complex access to a range of services, and means that communication between professionals and the interaction between treatment modalities is easier to manage. A single point of contact, and a coordinator of care that provides

Figure 9.4: CSCI rating – help to live at home for mental health service users

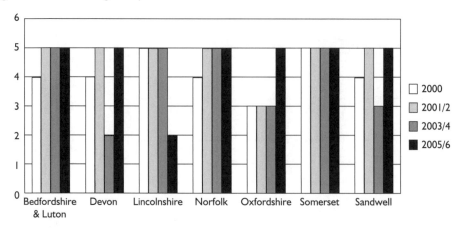

the information and ensures the service user voice is heard, adds to the integrated care experience.

The philosophy of this type of coordinated care is sound, and should result in a more effective and efficient provision of services to those in need, but in reality this is not always the case. The focus of both integrated provision and the care programme approach, which is central to the premise, is that each service user will have a care coordinator and a single care plan which will account for, and address, both health and social care needs. The therapeutic relationship between service user and worker has long been acknowledged as an important element within the experience (Holloway, 1991; Howgego et al., 2003; Buck and Alexander, 2006; Hewitt, 2005), and many service user groups have emphasised the impact of having a respectful and mutually valued working relationship as a key contributor to the recovery process.

This element is one which the patient surveys and the joint HCC/CSCI review examined. Nationally the rate of service users who knew who their care coordinator was varied from 39 per cent to 95 per cent across services, with an average of 70 per cent (HCC/CSCI 2006). Figure 9.5 demonstrates the findings from the patient surveys.

It appears from the patient survey data that the identification and availability of the designated care coordinator has remained stable over the past four years. The profession of the care coordinator may now differ, but the accessibility does not. The care programme approach (CPA) guidance (DoH, 1991; 1999a) is that all service users subject to CPA should have an identified care coordinator, yet approximately 30 per cent of service users are still not either aware of who is overseeing their care or are not receiving the services they require; this is not dependent upon the mode of service delivery (i.e. secondment or full integration), and remains an area that requires attention in terms of service improvement.

Figure 9.5: Identification and availability of care coordinators (per cent)

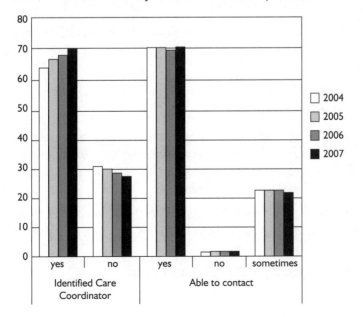

I feel I should be able to contact someone . . . I have felt so alone at times.
(Service user, quoted in HCC 2004 Patient Survey)

I just want to be safe in the knowledge that when I ask for help I'll get it.
(Service user, 2003, quoted at www.madnotbad.co.uk)

One criticism of the patient survey in terms of care coordination is that it focuses upon quantitative rather qualitative information. The emphasis is placed upon identification of the designated care coordinator and the ability to contact that individual. While these are undoubtedly important elements of the provision of coordinated and integrated care, how the professional communicates, and the quality of the therapeutic relationship, is of equal importance when considering the effectiveness of care and treatment.

I do need someone to help me. I really do. But I also need to feel in control, like I have a say. To have it recognised that I am the authority on my internal mental states.
(Service user, 2003, quoted at www.madnotbad.co.uk)

Historically, mental health service users have been passive recipients of care (Barnes and Shardlow, 1997; Peck et al., 2002), but this has changed over the past decade with an increasing emphasis, especially within social care, upon self-determination and empowerment. The nature of the service user–worker relationship needs to reflect this shift, and at present there is still an over-reliance on data, rather than experience, to define whether a service or profession is meeting the needs of the consumers of the service.

Question

To what extent are service user and carer voices heard within your local services?

The service user–worker relationship

As already stated one of the key themes throughout the literature is the development of a mutually respectful and trusting relationship between the service user and his or her care coordinator.

The ideal situation is much more to do with recognition and respect.
(Carer, quoted in Rethink, 2005)

This element of care provision is not dependent upon the organisational structure, or whether the employer is health- or social care-led, but is interlinked with organisational culture, and the professional boundaries discussed in Chapters 3 and 4 therefore do have the potential to impact upon the service user experience.

A study undertaken by Rethink in 2005 suggested that integrated working was still an ideal rather than a reality and reported that this was having an impact on the services received on the front line.

The thought is there . . . but the reality doesn't meet the concept.
(Carer, quoted in Rethink, 2005)

Carers in particular can find themselves devalued by services (Taylor and Barling, 2004; Brown and Smith, 1989), and often report feeling dismissed or even assessed as part of their relative's pathology.

Health and social care integration and carers

Social care as an approach views the individual as part of his or her social context, and concepts such as carer support, family work and involvement in the assessment and care planning process are integral to the work. Health colleagues, on the other hand, have no such emphasis in their approach, and often overlook the impact of the social support networks and environment on the health and well-being of the service user.

The emphasis of integrated care is that all services become more holistic, with health professionals considering social context and social care professionals considering health issues within both the assessment and provision of care. The principle is that mental health occurs within a wide biopsychosocial context which can only be addressed with partnership between service users, professions and providers, which then enables care provision that is more effective and meets the needs of the service user population.

> *Leading health and social care bodies will have got it right when they realise the future is working together.* (Carer and user of mental health services, Shropshire and Telford Service User Involvement Group, www.well-scrambled.co.uk)

Partnership with service users

Additionally, the issue of partnership with service users is an area that is yet to be fully addressed within provision (Moreland, 2007; Rogers et al., 1997; Rutter et al., 2004; Truman and Raine, 2002), and professional approaches are still having an impact upon the service user experience, as noted by Moreland in 2007 as part of the BBC Action Network mental health campaign:

> *Unless we are truly integrated into the professionals' very existence as part of normal life, we will always have a situation of them and us, causing the all too familiar faces of stigma and discrimination from the very people who should know better.* (Moreland, 2007)

Many service users are not aware of the integration process in terms of detail – their main concern is that they are able to access the care and support that they need. The morale of front line workers is an issue (Edwards et al., 2000; Cherniss and Egnatios, 1978) and has a direct impact upon the quality of services received, but the employing organisation is not an issue in itself.

Reflection point

If the professional background of the care coordinator is not the most important aspect for the service user, is the importance the worker often places upon it appropriate or relevant to the provision of quality care?

Figure 9.6: Case study example – Sarah

Sarah has been using mental health services for ten years; she has a diagnosis of schizo-affective disorder, and has had a number of psychotic and manic episodes which have led to hospital admission.

She has six-monthly outpatient appointments with her consultant psychiatrist who monitors her mental health and provides a prescribing regime. Sarah also sees her care coordinator weekly; she has had both a psychiatric nurse and a social worker as her care coordinator in the past.

Sarah rates the ability to talk to her coordinator and to feel listened to as the most important element of her care package; she does not know what profession her current care coordinator is, and states she does not really care.

The impact of organisational culture

One of the issues often raised by workers is the differences in organisational culture; this is especially the case with social care workers operating within NHS organisations. The identity of the social services department, with its collaborative and negotiative style of operation, is something that is comfortable for many social workers. The shift to hierarchical and auto-cratic management systems, by which the NHS is often characterised (Todd, 2002), has the potential to create a shock reaction when integration first occurs, regardless of the model of partnership applied. This aspect of integration has, in many areas, had a direct impact upon the morale and ethos of the social care workforce. It is an element that is key in terms of improving the service user experience.

A demoralised and de-motivated workforce is less likely to provide an empathic and respon-sive service to those in need, and the process of integration of health and social care thus needs to consider not only systems, process and perspectives, but also the personal and professional impact upon the individuals employed within the field.

Integration leading to disintegration

While the emphasis has been on the integration of health and social care agencies in the delivery of mental health care, little consideration has been given to what happens to the links between specialisms within a social services department. While social care staff and services have become more embedded within NHS services, they have moved further away from their social care colleagues who are still operating within local authority structures.

There has been significant discussion over the past two decades (Ellis et al., 1999; Charlis and Ferlie, 1987; Cambridge et al., 2005) regarding the move from generic adult and children's departments to service user specific services. A whole group of service users are unable to access support because while they are undoubtedly vulnerable, they do not quite fit the admission criteria of any area of provision.

The legislation in this area makes no distinction between the causes of need, and the definition of vulnerable within the NHS and Community Care Act 1990 is taken from the National Assistance Act of 1948. It states that a person is vulnerable as a result of requiring care or attention due to 'age, disability, illness or other circumstances' (section 42). In addition the 1990 Act places a duty on local authority services that requires them to make an assessment of any individual who meets the definition of vulnerability:

> *where it appears to a local authority that any person for whom they may provide or arrange for the provision of community care services may be in need of any such services, the authority –*
>
> *(a) shall carry out an assessment of his needs for those services; and*
>
> *(b) having regard to the results of that assessment, shall then decide whether his needs call for the provision by them of any such services.* (section 47; NHSCCA 1990).

While the partnership agreements that have created integrated mental health services include delegated statutory responsibility, there is not always a service available to meet the assessed need, and this is creating difficulties.

Personality disorder is a key example of this phenomenon. While an individual presenting to services with this condition may undoubtedly be vulnerable and in need of community care services, the community mental health services, which are still very often health-led, may be unable or unwilling to offer appropriate services to meet the need as the condition is not considered to be a severe mental illness. As there are no longer generic adult services, and the development of complex needs services, driven by the Department of Health guidelines *Personality Disorder: No Longer a Diagnosis of Exclusion* (NIMHE, 2003) is in many areas still in its infancy, this group of individuals may only be able to access services when they are in chaos or crisis, which is contrary to the policy direction of preventative measures (DoH, 2006).

It is often the case that when an individual with a personality disorder presents to a CMHT, conflict between health staff and social care staff is created. Whereas the medical and health staff can rely on the service criteria and medical 'treatability' to determine whether any provision is offered, social care staff are governed by community care legislation and policy, which states that the individual is vulnerable and that an assessment of need and sub-sequent care package should be considered.

This situation creates many difficulties within multi-disciplinary teams, and in some areas social workers are carrying caseloads of chaotic individuals, who may not be supported by any other professionals due to the diagnostic criteria in place within psychiatric services.

The linkage between mental health services and other social services departments is not as robust as it once was (Petch, 2007), and as a result, while individuals with mental health issues are now able to access health and social care services in one place, other needs – for example physical health, cultural needs, learning disabilities and housing – may not be as easily met.

The case of Steven (Figure 9.7) is not unusual: individuals in need rarely have just the one issue, and often the presenting needs span a range of health, social care, cultural and environmental areas.

Figure 9.7: Case study example – Steven

Steven is a 29-year-old Bengali man diagnosed with borderline personality disorder and a mild learning disability (IQ 69). His parents migrated to the UK prior to his birth and Steven has dual nationality.

Steven lives with his parents and younger brother (who is 17 and at sixth-form college). He went to mainstream schools and left at 16 with no qualifications. He entered a youth training apprenticeship in upholstery but did not complete this.

Steven's first contact with mental health services occurred when he was 18 years old; he had become involved with the local drug culture and he reported experiencing rapid mood swings and auditory hallucinations. He has been assessed in the past by learning disability services and was deemed as borderline and not in need of services.

Five years ago, following a period of increased mental instability resulting from excessive alcohol and stimulant use, Steven was assessed under the Mental Health Act 1983 and detained on a section 2 with suspected drug-induced psychosis. He was admitted to an acute psychiatric ward, but it soon became evident that he was very vulnerable due to his learning disabilities and that the acute unit was not an appropriate place for him. As a result he was transferred to a learning disability unit within the same health authority.

Steven's mental health state stabilised within a few weeks and he was discharged. On discharge he was followed up for a six-week period by a community learning disability nurse, but was not accepted into community social care learning disability services as he was assessed as borderline learning disability with primary mental health needs and thus not eligible for community services. Since then Steven's parents have cared for him without support from any services.

Three months ago Steven's mental health again began to deteriorate, which led to an increase in behavioural difficulties; his parents are finding it increasingly difficult to cope with him in the home. The police have been called out twice to deal with violent outbursts.

Local mental health services have conducted an assessment and are of the opinion that while Steven requires medication to maintain stability, in his mental health state this would be best provided in a primary care setting; and that his primary needs are behavioural, linked to his borderline learning disability.

Learning disability services also carried out an assessment and stated that the learning disability is supplementary and not the primary issue or cause of his need, and as such are not able to provide support. Steven is not substance-dependent or wishing to change his drug-using behaviour (which he states is occasional and recreational in nature) and local substance misuse services therefore have little to offer him.

Consequently, at the time of writing Steven's parents are not able to access appropriate services via the statutory sector, though they do receive support from a local carers' group and Steven attends the MIND day centre. These services are a great help to the family but are not able to provide the level of care that Steven's vulnerability creates.

The family have reached crisis point and are not able to maintain the situation. Following an incident in 2008, when Steven attacked his younger brother, they are now stating that Steven needs to leave the family home.

Questions
What options would be available for Steven in your local area?
Should services be offered to support Steven regardless of the ability to make significant changes to his situation?

The integration of health and social care within mental health provision is one of the strategies developed to close the so-called 'gaps' in service, but this has not been delivered quite as originally envisioned. Previous chapters have highlighted issues such as differing professional perspectives and models of operation; this chapter suggests that differing legislative frameworks and specialist service criteria and cultures also contribute to the difficulties in achieving true integration of service delivery, and each of these has a direct impact upon the service user experience of services.

The service user perspective: what difference has integration made?

The initial quotation for this chapter was taken from the 2000 Department of Health publication *The NHS Plan*, which highlighted the aims of integrating health and social care with mental health care provision. These aims were centred upon the service user experience, simplifying pathways and improving access, by joining together the range of provisions necessary in the drive towards effectiveness and quality improvement across care services.

It appears that while in some areas the integration of services has been deemed successful, this has not necessarily improved the service user experience, and in some cases has created a different 'gap' for individuals to fall down.

Patient surveys, while useful, do not provide the full story: the majority of the additional evaluation and evidence in this area is anecdotal and local in nature, and so does not provide the evidence for a national picture on the effectiveness and success of the integration of services.

In some areas the partnerships originally established under section 31 of the Health Act 1999 are now being dissolved as there is a concern that the NHS is not an appropriate or able body to provide social care. National surveys, such as Dame Denise Platt's 2006 evaluation *The State of Social Care*, appear to support the view that social care in mental health services has not improved as a result of integrated provision.

Much of the evidence regarding the service user's experience of mental health services (and indeed social care services overall) relates to the value placed upon the client–worker relationship. Issues such as feeling listened to and valued, and a partner in the care process, are highlighted as the key considerations. From the service users' perspective it does not much matter who employs their key-worker, or which professional group that worker comes from.

It appears that the integration process, while initially coming from a service user and carer perspective and designed to improve services and create an ease of access, has in some cases failed to deliver these aims. Instead there has been a concentration on organisational change and service specifications, which has made little real difference to those who depend upon health and social care services as part of their daily lives.

Further reading

Health Care Commission and Commission for Social Care Inspection (2007) *No Voice, No Choice: A joint review of adult community mental health services in England*. London: HCC.

Rethink (2005) *Future Perfect: Mental Health Service Users Set Out a Vision for the 21st Century*. Available via Rethink (www.rethink.co.uk).

Chapter 10

Approved Mental Health Professionals: a Trojan horse?

If you open that Pandora's Box . . . who knows what Trojan [h]orses will jump out.
(Ernest Bevin, 1881–1951)

PQ framework

Achieving Post-qualifying Social Work awards

This chapter will assist in the meeting of National Occupational Standards for Social Work:

Key Role 2, Unit 9:   Address behaviour which presents a risk to individuals, families, carers, groups, and communities.

Key Role 4, Unit 13:   Assess, minimise and manage risk to self and colleagues.

For registered social workers considering, or working towards, post-qualifying awards, this chapter will also assist in meeting the requirements of both the specialist award in mental health and the national occupational standards in mental health, which are core to the post-qualification standards in this area.

MHNOS 44:   Promote peoples' rights and encourage them to recognise their responsibilities.

MHNOS 79:   Enable workers and agencies to work collaboratively.

PQ Specialist Award in Mental Health

47 (ii)   Applying knowledge, understanding and skill in relevant legal and policy frameworks.

47 (xi)   Influencing and supporting communities, organisations, agencies and services to promote peoples' mental health.

Introduction

The Approved Social Worker (ASW) role, which was enshrined within the Mental Health Act 1983, has become an integral part of social work within mental health services. The amendments to the Mental Health Act introduced by the Mental Health (Amendment) Act 2007 are the first major shifts towards inclusion of other professional groups within the formal mental health system. The proposals in regard to updating and modernising mental health law were originally commenced in 1998 when the government commissioned a review of the legislation. This was as a result of changing policy in regard to service delivery, and it thus became necessary to review and update the legislative framework to make it relevant to current practice.

This chapter concentrates on the role of the ASW, soon to be Approved Mental Health Professional (AMHP), in an attempt to consider some of the implications facing professional groups outside social work who will be undertaking the role. While the initial implementation of the Mental Health (Amendment) Act 2007 will be to convert existing ASW staff into AMHPs, the opportunity for nurses, occupational therapists and psychologists to become AMHPs will be available from the latter half of 2008, and these groups will therefore need to consider what this will mean for their practice and their professional perspectives.

The sufficiency of ASW staff has long been a concern across local authorities. The 1983 Act placed a duty on local authority areas to provide 'sufficient' numbers of ASWs to provide a 24-hour service (s 114). A survey carried out by the ASW Leads Network in 2006 found that between 17 per cent (non-London) and 60 per cent (inner and outer London) of boroughs surveyed reported that they had sufficient numbers of ASW staff to meet the needs of their areas. One particular concern in relation to ASW provision is that of an ageing workforce (ADSS, 2006); the introduction of the AMHP enables other professions to take on the statutory role within mental health service provision, and potentially expands the availability and perspectives of the workforce.

The following discussion presents the social work view of the expanding role. The ASW workforce, while welcoming other professions into what has traditionally been a social work domain, are concerned about the ability of medical and allied health professions to continue the tradition of independence from the medical model of mental health care. This independence is a key factor in ensuring that the holistic consideration of patients' rights and needs is undertaken, and the precarious balance between care and control is maintained.

Mental health legislation review and the modernisation agenda

As discussed in Chapter 2, the policy agenda for mental health services has seen a significant shift over the past 15 years. This has resulted in the blurring of the boundaries of traditional professional roles in favour of a core set of generic competencies and capabilities underpinning the skills and knowledge that each profession group contributes to the multidisciplinary team and subsequent service provision. The aim is not to make all professions the same, but to maximise the commonalities to promote co-working that will benefit the service users.

Despite the general consensus that mental health legislation in the UK was in need of review, the process has been fraught with controversy. The overall view was that service provision was changing to reflect the social inclusion and well-being agendas, with competency and evidence-based practice being promoted across all professions, and the legislative framework needed to reflect this. An additional consideration within this review was the long-term sustainability of the existing provisions. The sufficiency of ASW staff has been highlighted as an issue since the early 1990s (Huxley and Kerfoot, 1994; ADSS, 2006), and the workforce is ageing, with an average age of ASWs being mid-50s (ADSS, 2006) and a lack of recruitment into the role to replace these staff (Huxley et al., 2005). With this being the case action was needed to ensure that the statutory duties conferred by the Mental Health Act could continue to be effectively delivered.

The first set of proposals was published in 1999 with the subsequent draft bill published in 2002. These were met with widespread criticism, mainly focused upon what were termed 'draconian' powers that emphasised risk to the public, rather than individual need. After much debate this version of the bill was dropped. In 2004 the second edition of the Mental Health Bill was published; this too was met with debate and criticism. While there was a general agreement that the proposed reform was needed, the 2004 bill was seen as complicated and unwieldy and this too was retracted.

In 2006 the final version of the Mental Health Bill was published; this time the government opted for a series of amendments to the 1983 Act. These concentrated on streamlining the legislation and mirroring the reforms that had already been introduced across mental health services. The key changes in terms of the professional roles are illustrated in Figure 10.1. This chapter is not seeking to provide a full overview of the amendments to the Mental Health Act, and readers are directed to the Mental Health Act 2007 and the associated code of practice for full details.

The actual operation of the AMHP and Responsible Clinician roles is still being developed and guidance is being issued. The first task in the implementation of the new legislation is to undertake the conversion of the current ASW workforce into AMHPs. The Responsible Clinician role will require approval under section 12, as for the current Responsible Medical Officer (RMO), and competencies and guidance are yet to be published.

Figure 10.1: Key changes to professional roles

> - Approved Clinicians and Responsible Clinicians – roles defined and expanded beyond medical practitioners (clauses 11–19: amended s 12).
> - Approved Mental Health Professionals (AMHPs) to replace the Approved Social Worker – similar in operation and responsibility to the ASW but enables other professions to undertake the role (clauses 20–24: amended s 6, s 13 and s 114).
> - Other amendments that are relevant to the new roles are:
>
>   ○ The treatability clause has been amended and now states – 'medical treatment the purpose of which is to alleviate or prevent a worsening of the disorder or one of its symptoms or manifestations' (clause : amended s 3 and s 58);
>   ○ Approval by a Second Opinion Appointed Doctor (SOAD) can now be given if 'it is appropriate that the treatment is given' (clause 6: amended s 58 and s 57).

○ Medical treatment is defined as including 'nursing, psychological intervention and specialist mental health habilitation, rehabilitation and care' (clause 9: s 145).
○ Advocacy services for detained service users.
○ Nearest relatives – service users can now apply for displacement.
○ The introduction of Community Treatment Orders.

The General Social Care Council (GSCC) issued draft competencies for the AMHP role in January 2008. These are very similar to the original ASW competencies and it seems that other professional groups undertaking the role will be required to demonstrate both an understanding of the social model of mental distress, and also an application of the social welfare value base, in order to become 'approved'.

The independence of the AMHP role remains a concern, and as a result local authorities will retain the duty of approval, as they have done with the ASW role. This will remain the case regardless of the professional background or employer of those who become AMHPs under the amended Act.

Multi-professional approval in mental health law

While the inclusion of other professions is a new development in the UK, other countries have had such a system for many years; for example, in Australia, under their 1986 Mental Health Act, nurses, psychologists, social workers and occupational therapists are all able to undertake the Mental Health Practitioner role with appropriate and approved training.

The updated mental health legislation is in line with the modernisation agenda and the integration of services which has been developing since the inception of community care. The aim is that services are staffed based on skill mix and competencies required to meet the needs of the users, rather than on professional background. While this is the overall strategy, there are still significant discrepancies in the training programmes and requirements for the different professional groups, and there is a clear distinction (and at times conflict) in the perspective that each profession brings to service delivery. These varying perspectives can be beneficial to the user of services, as there is potential for a more holistic assessment of presenting needs, but the professional divides discussed in Chapters 3 and 4 do not always facilitate this.

If the legal framework is to expand effectively to be more inclusive and enable autonomy in roles for disciplines other than medical practitioners and social workers, there will need to be consideration of how to maintain and develop this within the context of the variety of power relationships that can (and do) exist between the different disciplines.

Independence and autonomy

One of the concerns that was raised by the ASW workforce, and in particular the British Association of Social Workers (BASW), related to the issue of independence and autonomy. The main element of the ASW role has historically been that of independence from the medical profession, based on human rights and social justice principles.

The process of undertaking ASW training for social workers begins when they first start their social work qualification, which is value-based and directly related to the exercise of statutory duties. As these workers enter their ASW specific training they come equipped with foundation knowledge and post-qualification experience. The role of specialist ASW training is to provide an intensive overview of mental health law and the implications attached to undertaking these duties. The concern raised regarding other professions entering the role is that foundation training and experience are not necessarily based on social justice principles and in many cases are directly related to the medical model framework. The ASW role has traditionally maintained objectivity and independence from the medical perspective. This ensures that the best interests and rights of the client are observed, despite the power imbalances that can occur between service users and professionals.

AMHP training

A key element within the AMHP role is that of training provision. The legislation continues to place local authorities as the responsible authority in terms of both training and providing sufficient numbers of competent staff. This retains the independence from the NHS that is required if the role is to be autonomous and based on the social model. In addition to this provision, the AMHP competencies are to mirror the original ASW competencies, which consider a whole range of skills and knowledge required to exercise mental health act duties effectively. This includes holistic consideration of all the circumstances of an individual's case beyond those of diagnosis and compliance with treatment, which, although they are crucial to the assessment process, are only one element of the complexity of a person's biopsychosocial functioning and mental state.

The regulation of the AMHP training requirements will be maintained by the General Social Care Council (GSCC) as is presently the case for ASW training. This will have a significant impact upon other professions, as they will be required to maintain a commitment to the GSCC code of practice as well as their own professional bodies. While there are commonalities to all professional groups in terms of ethics and basic practice principles, there are key differences in terms of theoretical understanding and evidence base. There are many opportunities for the social work profession within the development of the AMHP, and the current ASWs have a definite leadership role within the change process to ensure that the perspective is not subsumed within the medical model of treatment. How this will work within practice is yet to be determined, but there is a precedent for the model which has been created by the formation of partnership trusts.

Setting the precedent – ASWs employed by the NHS

The concerns relating to ASW independence and autonomy had already begun to be voiced as a result of the Health Act 1999, which saw some authorities transferring the ASW workforce into the employ of NHS Trusts (as discussed in Chapters 5 and 6). The arrangement in these cases were that while the NHS were the employers of the ASW staff, the local authorities retained the authority to appoint and warrant ASWs, and while exercising their duties the ASWs were acting on behalf of the local authority social services department rather than their direct employers. This separation of management and professional activity is well established within health environments, but for social care staff it is a very different model of operation and has created discomfort. The new AMHP role will mirror these arrangements, and while exercising statutory duties the AMHP will be acting on behalf of, and with accountability to, the local authority. In some cases the service will be operationally delivered within partnership NHS Trusts. This arrangement is possible, as already demonstrated, but it will require clear statements of responsibility, accountability and practice standards in order to be applied effectively and according to current evidence.

Reflection point

Consider accountability and responsibility – how would you manage this duality within your practice?

Power and powerlessness

Power, and its usage, is a key issue within the ASW/AMHP role. It has been commented that the ASW is one of the most powerful civilian powers in existence within the UK, and this is a key consideration within the training that the professional undertakes. On the one hand there is a total power–powerlessness imbalance between the ASW and the service user, and on the other hand the ASW must take all actions necessary to consider the service user's views and wishes. This is a difficult balance to achieve and the issue remains that while there is a clear rationale for opening the role to a range of professional groups, caution is required to ensure that this balance is maintained and that professionals undertaking the role are able to step back from the usual service and professional issues and act in an independent, holistic and evidence-based manner. Figure 10.2 illustrates the potential range of issues, pressures and dilemmas that the ASW may face when operating within the statutory role.

Figure 10.2: Case study example – Mrs L

Background

Mrs L is a 38-year-old Asian female. She is married and has two children aged 3 and 7. Her husband is an active member of the local Muslim community and views his wife's responsibilities as staying at home and looking after their children. Mr L's parents and two brothers live locally and Mrs L has a good relationship with her mother-in-law but does not get on with her male relatives who she sees as judging her in terms of her parenting skills. Mrs L's first language is Punjabi; however, she is fluent in English.

Mrs L first became ill following the birth of her second child when she experienced a severe case of post-natal depression which resulted in her admission to the local acute mental health facility with psychotic symptoms. Since this time she has had one further admission under section 2 of the Mental Health Act 1983 due to delusional beliefs and paranoid ideation that centred on her husband threatening to remove the children from her care.

Current situation

Mrs L has been referred by her consultant psychiatrist who believes she is acutely unwell and has completed his medical recommendation prior to assessment by the ASW and second doctor. On attending Mrs L's home it appears that she is very angry: Mr L tells you that he and his wife are having marital problems due to her illness, and is concerned about the children. Mrs L is refusing to converse with you in English; you contact the translation service who state that they cannot supply an interpreter until 2pm the following day. The consultant psychiatrist wants Mrs L to be admitted today and has told Mr L that this will be the case.

Questions

- What additional information do you require and where would you get this?
- What are the risks present in this case?
- What are the power issues involved in this case?
- What would you do?

The ASW in the case in Figure 10.2 is potentially facing pressure from both family members and other professionals, and this is not an uncommon scenario. The social justice perspective allows the ASW to view the case in a holistic manner and ask the questions that are often not considered within medical terms, for example:

- What social supports are present?

- How much is the marital distress impacting upon Mrs L's presentation?

- What agendas are at play within the situation?

The legal status of the ASW role provides the worker with the authority to consider the available options outside the potential pressure that other views and agendas may create. This is an invaluable role for the service user (Gilbert, 2003), and the conversion to AMHP status and the inclusion of professionals other than social workers must ensure that this status and authority do not become degraded within professional or organisational politics.

Considerations with AMHP training

Professional training for all practitioners within mental health is now based upon essential shared capabilities (as discussed in Chapter 3) and the *New Ways of Working* document, which is currently being implemented across the country. These frameworks focus upon a core set of generic skills and will support the implementation of the AMHP role by providing a sound value base centred upon anti-discriminatory principles, from which operation and decision making can be derived. This is not to divert professions from their own identities, as Chapter 3 argued, but to build on core skill sets that are common to all and within which professional perspectives can be applied and practised. It is worth noting that the results of these changes will take time and will require performance management within organisations to ensure that they are being appropriately applied.

The AMHP will be required to continue the tradition of applying the 'least restrictive option' and there will thus be a significant learning curve for some health professionals entering the role, to ensure that their awareness of community options and community care legislation is in place. Figure 10.3 demonstrates the range of considerations that are made by the ASW/ AMHP as core elements of the assessment process. This illustration is not intended to be a comprehensive guide to what issues and considerations should feature within an assessment under the Mental Health Act, as each case poses its own set of issues and challenges. The aim here is to provide an overview of the scope of possible influences within the process.

The ASW/AMHP is required to coordinate the process as a whole, and the 2007 Act maintains this role. Professionals entering into AMHP training, and subsequently undertaking the role, therefore need to be aware of the whole range of influences and options that have traditionally been integral to the social work perspective.

It is also the case that the changes to the responsible medical officer (RMO) role, into a multi-professional responsible clinician (RC) role, could also be subject to the same discussions, and consideration needs to be given to the social work profession's engagement with this new role. While there is undoubtedly an argument that, in some cases, a social worker may be the most appropriate professional to undertake the RC role in some cases – for example for community-based service users who are in receipt of social care services – the actual exercising of the role will require significant considerations. Some initial considerations are as follows:

Figure 10.3: Factors that require consideration within MHA assessment

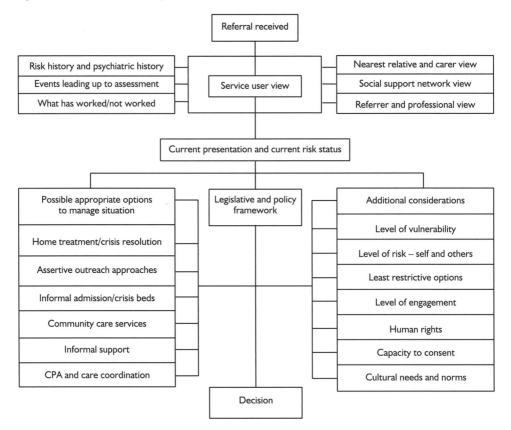

- What relationship exists between the RC and the consultant psychiatrist, and how will the decision making and accountability for patient care be apportioned?

- Can a social worker carry out both the AMHP and the RC roles, and if the potential conflict in roles cannot be resolved what implications will this have for the social work profession as a whole and specifically the ASW/AMHP workforce?

The code of practice for the Mental Health (Amendment) Act 2007 is, at the time of writing, available in draft form, and the application of new provisions will develop further as directions are issued and implementation is progressed. In the meantime all the professions involved in the care of detained patients need to remain aware of the whole range of impacts and considerations that are required to ensure an anti-discriminatory and value-based application of compulsory mental health treatment.

The Trojan horse?

This chapter began by stating that the expansion of the ASW role into the AMHP multi-professional role is potentially a Trojan horse, and it is not yet clear what 'Pandora's box' will be opened as a result. The first question to be answered is whether the inclusion of other professionals within the AMHP role is a positive step for modern mental health services. Despite the concerns regarding different models of practice and perspective. the resounding answer is yes. This is due to a number of factors, as illustrated in Figure 10.4.

The ASW workforce has been under significant pressure over recent years, with many authorities struggling to meet their statutory requirements in capacity terms (Huxley and Kerfoot, 1994; Huxley et al., 2005; ADSS, 2006). The actual benchmark in terms of sufficiency is one of national debate and varies dramatically across regions. Many localities have considered sufficiency within their own areas, and a report by the chair of the ASW leads network in 2006 also considered the issue. In most cases the measurement of what is sufficient is subjective, and the legal guidance of 'sufficient ASWs to cover a 24 hour, 7 day a week service' (Mental Health Act 1983) provides no further clarity.

Figure 10.4: Potential benefits of the multi-professional AMHP role

- Different perspectives available to contribute to the process of holistic assessment of needs;
- Increasing the number of available staff to undertake the statutory role;
- Reflects the policy agenda and development of services;
- Reflects the core skills principles;
- Provides access to high quality training to all staff groups;
- Consistent professional development and career progression across mental health services;
- Cements the principles of human rights and risk assessment within all professions.

> **Reflection point**
>
> What is your view of a range of different professions taking on a traditional social work role?
>
> What is considered sufficient in your area?

Integration issues

The shift towards partnership trusts in some areas has made this difficulty all the more acute. Social services departments have become more unwilling to release staff from other services to undertake ASW roles due to the view that the mental health services are operationally responsible for this provision under partnership arrangements. This does not detract from the issue that local authorities are accountable for this provision; however, it does make it easier for authorities to look externally rather than internally for the required staff.

The AMHP role is partially a response to the increasing pressure that ASWs find themselves under as their numbers dwindle, but there is also the potential for injecting what have been traditional 'social care' values across other professional groups.

Areas such as self-determination and positive risk-taking are key examples of core considerations undertaken by the ASW, and a potential culture shift could therefore occur across service provision with other professions entering the statutory role. The agendas discussed in Chapter 2, social inclusion and recovery focused principles, are areas that over the past decade have been used as soundbites and buzzwords, but in terms of the delivery of care at the coal face, while there has been a culture shift this has not been at the same rapid pace as policy development. A range of factors such as theoretical understandings and professional identities, which have been discussed elsewhere in this book, are partially responsible for the lack of pace in the change process, and the shift in legislation is the first statutory move to support what has been an identified policy direction for a significant period.

The AMHP role is potentially a valuable addition to the mental health workforce and a powerful ally to the social work profession. This is the first time that social work has been able to affect wholesale change with other professions. Although the policy direction and competency frameworks have been based upon social care values, there has been little actually to signify this, and the social care workforce has not taken the opportunity to lead. The ASWs, however, will not have the same ability to sit back and become passive recipients of change. The current workforce is expected to lead the process of training and accreditation of other professional groups, and will form the majority of the AMHP population for at least the first five years.

This being the case, a clear opportunity exists to ensure that social care values and principles remain at the forefront of mental health care and become a significant influence upon practice development across the range of professions and services.

Further reading

Association of Directors of Social Services (2006) *Survey of Approved Social Workers in England*. London: ADSS.

Huxley, P., Evans, E., Webber, M., and Gately, C. (2005) Staff shortages in the mental health workforce: the case of the disappearing approved social worker. *Health and Social Care in the Community*, 13 (6), 504–13.

Chapter 11
From the other angle: a word from health

By Dr Mehraj Shah and Dr Akeem Sule

What we see depends mainly on what we look for. (John Lubbock, 1839–1913)

PQ framework

Achieving Post-qualifying Social Work awards

This chapter will assist in the meeting of National Occupational Standards for Social Work:

Key Role 5, Unit 17:   Work within multi-disciplinary and multi-organisational teams, networks and systems.

Key Role 6, Unit 20:   Manage complex ethical issues, dilemmas and conflicts.

For registered social workers considering, or working towards, post-qualifying awards, this chapter will also assist in meeting the requirements of both the specialist award in mental health and the national occupational standards in mental health, which are core to the post-qualification standards in this area.

MHNOS 57:   Monitor, evaluate and improve processes for delivering mental health services to a population.

MHNOS 80:   Explore, initiate and improve processes for developing collaborative working relationships.

PQ Specialist Award in Mental Health

47 (vii)   Working collaboratively with other professions.

47 (x)   Utilising appropriate knowledge and research from other disciplines.

Foreword by Daisy Bogg

This chapter has been written by two medical colleagues, Dr Mehraj Shah and Dr Akeem Sule, both of whom work within the eastern region of England in an integrated partnership mental health trust. The aim of including different perspectives within this text is to provide a balance to the social work perspective. The perspective of the medical profession is often in contrast to the social model, with an attention to biological rather than sociological approaches to mental distress, but in many instances doctors and social workers (especially ASWs) have close and collaborative working relationships. There is a requirement on both professions to cooperate within legal and clinical situations, in order to provide the best possible treatment for the service users who access services. Social care often forgets that the issue of integration is far reaching and has an impact on health colleagues as well as the social work profession, and this account is included to ensure that, as part of the consideration of the impact of integrated care, social workers are encouraged to look beyond their experiences and consider the implications from another perspective.

The coverage of power differentials, theoretical grounding and policy discussions in this book have considered the medical view; however, these issues have been seen from the perspective of social care, whereas this chapter is written from a medical perspective by medical professionals. Elements of this perspective can be difficult and challenging for the social work profession, but this does not detract from the validity of the views expressed and it is important to be aware of how other professional groups view social work within modern mental health services.

Introduction

Over the past 50 years, mental health professionals in general, and psychiatrists in particular, have increasingly recognised the distinctive strengths of the contribution of social work to modern mental health. The contribution of social work knowledge, skills and values is integral to the reform, and to the future of, mental health services. The role of social workers has been growing with the modernisation of mental health services. The closure of mental health institutions in the 1980s, led to an increased emphasis on the promotion of independence and social integration of patients with mental illness, and thus increased the need for social care.

Social workers are currently an integral part of community mental health teams (CMHTs), and the only mental health workers with social science training. This encompasses a wide range of theoretical perspectives and methods of intervention, underpinned by participative approaches, anti-oppressive practice and the principles of social inclusion. This knowledge informs the contribution that practitioners and managers make to mental health services, within their core statutory responsibilities. It is also a significant contributory factor to effective multi-disciplinary working and to effective organisational development and improvement (Gilbert, 2003).

The National Health Service (NHS) has been changing and evolving ever since it came into existence. In the recent past the changes have been so rapid that the NHS is now the fastest changing health service in the world. The speed of change has resulted in an increasing cynicism among NHS employees, including doctors.

The accounts that follow are not necessarily views shared by the authors, but do represent a cross-section of medical views and opinions from doctors operating within integrated service provision.

Methodology

While preparing for writing this chapter we aimed to explored the clinicians' viewpoint from their experience of yet another change in the NHS: the integration of social services with mental health trusts. To do this a number of medical colleagues were approached and asked to comment on their experiences of integration and joint working – and the responses, as expected, were mixed. These ranged from highly optimistic and positive to total indifference.

For the purposes of this chapter, practicing clinicians within the eastern region of England were approached. All those surveyed were employed within integrated mental health trusts, and the doctors surveyed were at various levels of training, expertise and responsibilities, ranging from senior house officers on rotation, through to consultant psychiatrists and clinical directors.

The views expressed are in no way a reflection of doctors throughout the country, but do serve to provide some understanding of how doctors perceive the integration of health and social care provision, and represents a snapshot of the medical experience of partnership working in practice.

A snap shot

Interestingly, it appears that the most optimistic and enlightened views are from some of the senior consultants, many of whom are also involved in management. One comment stated that:

> *in order to understand the relationship between the mental health and social care we need to go back to basics of our psychiatric knowledge.*
> (Consultant psychiatrist, Bedfordshire)

The foundation of psychiatric understanding is that mental illnesses are multi-factorial in origin. Genetic and environmental interplay is the most popular way of explaining the phenomenon, but stress is almost always related to causation, and the result is a mental illness.

Developing a mental illness commonly leads to social difficulties, such as housing problems, financial difficulties, and relationship and employment problems. The perspective of many of those clinicians surveyed was that the way to address these issues is with the help of social worker. Social problems can be either the cause or the effect of mental illness; the treatment is therefore not only medical and psychological but social as well.

Although provision of mental health care and social work has traditionally been closely linked, there was in the past a distinction between the mental health team, comprising medical and nursing staff, who would deal with mental illness, and the social worker, who would deal with the social issues. This situation resulted in a lack of continuity of care, as each professional group worked independently and often was unaware of the other's actions and recommendations.

From the point of view of care delivery, this created a disjointed and uncoordinated approach, which often had a direct impact upon the effectiveness of services provided:

I don't believe in models be it medical, social or working models, we need a holistic approach. (Senior psychiatric consultant)

This perspective has been recognised at all levels in the medical hierarchy and is possibly one of the most important reasons for recent changes in the training of doctors.

Changes in training have happened at graduate and postgraduate levels. The preferred approach now encompasses biological, psychological and social perspectives, compared to the old model where the biological perspective was the central element of learning. With this being the case, present trainees are more alert to the social needs of patients.

I honestly believe that social worker's knowledge and skill should be involved right from the beginning of the training of medical students. (Staff grade psychiatrist)

Partnership working can facilitate this type of cross-fertilisation within training and contribute to the effectiveness of multi-disciplinary operation across all professions. A greater understanding of the perspective and function of the different professions can ease the integration process, as confusions between roles, responsibilities and expectations are more easily addressed if tackled within the training phase of each individual discipline.

The advantages of integration

Recent policy suggests that the best way forward to address the issue of uncoordinated service responses is integration. The advantages of this are undoubtedly multi-dimensional for clinicians and patients alike. It has made the overall practice within mental health care more holistic, making it possible to address the full range of issues, both social and medical.

One of the key advantages of partnership care is that of community-based approaches. The additional support available within the community has been shown to enhance the experience of service users, as the opportunity to maintain people at home for as long as possible means that hospital admissions, which can be traumatic and counterproductive for some patients, can be minimised.

The principle of integration means that the creation of a one-stop shop is a future possibility. This would make the access to mental health care more streamlined, with access to specialist and comprehensive assessment, as well as direct interventions and care, for both service users and their carers.

Benefits of partnership

From a medical perspective, one of the key points highlighted among those surveyed was the advantage of operating within a multi-disciplinary team. The sharing of skills, resources and knowledge, and an increased opportunity for networking, are integral to day-to-day practice and professional development, and are considered by medical professionals as valuable aspects of integrated working. The result of this is a potential increase in the speed at which services can be accessed, which thus ensures a quicker response for patients/carers.

In material terms, partnership is often financially beneficial as it has the potential to increase the economies of scale, and is more cost-effective compared to the traditional model of inpatient wards. More options for treatment become available as part of this process, and there are increased opportunities for coordinated care to ensure seamless provision between the home and hospital, depending upon the needs and risks presented.

It is considered by medical colleagues that the joint system is more efficient than the more historical uni-professional models, and reduces duplication through joint assessment, documentation and identification of both health and social care needs within one system.

The operation of partnership care is now more normalised across service systems, and as this is becoming more the case, a less institutionalised form of care is developing. This move may potentially contribute to the reduction of the associated stigma and prejudices that the mental health label can bring, especially as the development of mental health promotion and prevention is continued within more mainstream settings.

Overall the perspective of the psychiatric community suggests that partnership is galvanising, and with it a door is being opened to a shared vision of the future direction of mental health services for the people in need.

The social presentation of patients

The clinical presentation of patients has changed over the decades, a factor which is probably related to changes in the social system. Society has evolved in such a way that social needs have been increasingly recognised as the precipitating, causative and maintaining factors of mental illness. With this being the case social needs, if not addressed, may lead directly to the delay in implementation of an effective treatment and management plan.

One key example would be in the case of delayed discharge from hospital, in which the implementation of the recovery model is not possible until the patient has somewhere to live. Doctors and nurses have now recognised the fact that social work knowledge and skills are important within all aspects of patient care, and it is now expected that partnership trusts should be able to deliver high quality care in a holistic and integrated manner, which fully accounts for all the presenting needs regardless of perspective or discipline.

Models of service delivery

Home treatment and assertive outreach teams have increasingly recognised that social needs are one of the most significant factors for both relapse and maintenance of mental ill health. There has been little social work input into home treatment teams from the outset, but with integration, this deficiency in the provision of care is expected to be addressed.

It has been noted that in the eastern region, social workers are very well integrated into Assertive Outreach Teams (AOTs); in one area this was established prior to the partnership trust coming into existence. The client group of this team has complex needs, of both a biological and social nature. The role of social workers has not only been recognised by the other members of team in this area, but also by the patients, their families and carers.

I believe that the improved outcomes for the complex patient group that the assertive outreach team serve, is largely due to good integration of social workers within the multi-disciplinary care environment. (AOT consultant psychiatrist)

The AOT consultant went on to say that with trusts now becoming full partnerships; he is expecting that similar outcomes will become evident within the crisis and home treatment teams.

Recovery and the medical perspective

One key area of agreement between medical and social work colleagues is that symptom relief is not the recovery from illness, although definition of what recovery actually is differs. The medical view sees full recovery as going back to pre-morbid functioning, that is being able to function in society in the same way the person used to before getting ill, whereas the social work view places the service user's definition of recovery at the core of its meaning.

Regardless of the differences in understanding, the experience in AOT has widened both professions' outlooks and horizons, and facilitated the questioning and challenging of how each discipline views the term 'recovery'. The impact upon the medical profession has been that there is an increased willingness to consider recovery not only in medical terms, but also in social terms. The hope is that with continued integration, this holistic understanding will become the generalised view of patient care and recovery.

Medical expectations of integration

It has been increasingly recognised that sometimes the social situation is such that changes and alterations in it could lead to full recovery. With integration, medical practitioners increasingly expect social workers to identify such cases and manage them, thus reducing the workload of other colleagues in the team. This is not always the experience of the integrated teams, and social workers can at times be reluctant to take on this role.

Many consultants feel free to discuss a medical management with nursing colleagues, but have noticed the reluctance on the part of some social workers to engage in and contribute to such discussions. It may be that this is as a result of the lack of medical background; however, within an integrated environment there is an expectation that social workers will take a lead in learning from medical colleagues. This deficiency could be addressed by allowing social workers to work alongside nursing and medical colleagues within ward environments.

It is the view of medical practitioners that they are often more aware of the role and responsibilities of social workers, but that they in turn appear to know little about the medical aspects of mental health care. It is possible that partnership trusts can bridge this gap, but this has not yet been realised in practice.

The barriers to integrated working

A small number of psychiatrists surveyed, both senior and junior, were cynical about the partnership between social services and mental health. They felt that the contribution of this initiative was yet another layer of bureaucracy. They appeared to believe that it is now time to pause, and think about all the changes and so-called reforms that appear to be endlessly applied. In addition there is an increasing suspicion among some members of the medical profession regarding whether integration could be a significant factor in what is viewed as a conspiracy to undermine the medical profession.

Medical professionals are increasingly convinced that the NHS agenda is to de-professionalise doctors in general. The reasons for this shift are believed to be about power and control, and a wider political agenda concerning a focus on management and output driven services.

The changes in the structure, delivery and assessment of psychiatric training and the creation of new bodies with wide-ranging powers have led to multiple tiers of management. Medical colleagues consider the ethos of this to be that it is easier to exert control over non-professionals by using multiple layers and messages.

The underlying message is clear: politicians make changes by signalling that they know what is for the best. The psychiatrist surveyed as a result of this work also mentioned that *New Ways of Working* is being used to take traditional roles away from psychiatrists.

The aim of *New Ways of Working* is to share responsibility with the multi-disciplinary team, and hence leave the consultant to deal with the complex cases. However, a question which needs to be urgently addressed is how we train the trainees to deal with complex cases when they might have limited time and opportunity to do so.

> *I was integrated from the beginning as a part of the Community Mental Health Team. We have a high proportion of social workers and approved social workers in our team; they did not cause any untoward incidents in good working relationships in our Community Mental Health Team.* (Senior consultant)

For some of the clinicians, the integration of health and social care has made little difference in terms of working relationships or practices. There is recognition among medical professionals that the social work professionals were concerned about losing their autonomy and independence, and on this point the two are united: neither group wants to lose what it sees as its unique contribution.

Defining roles

The definition of roles is an area that still requires attention, and while there are definite commonalities in the work of all team members, there are also key areas of specialism that should be recognised and maintained. These include such areas as diagnosis and prescription of medication for medical staff and social support, housing, employment and involvement in social networks for the social work staff. Overall, however, the general view is that while such matters as team and individual worker responsibility, hierarchy and data collection all come under the aegis of one organisation, the delivery of streamlined and coordinated services is a clear benefit to all concerned.

One psychiatrist surveyed said that what has worked well so far is joint assessments between social workers and other members of team. This has enabled a learning process between disciplines, and is something which has been created by the integration of service delivery.

Although social workers and medical practitioners have undertaken joint assessments for two decades, this has been restricted to those carried out under the Mental Health Act 1983. Due to the integration of teams, this has now become a routine part of working practice. Professionals are now more able to undertake assessments of need quickly, and the carer's assessments are also more expedient than they once were. The co-location of professionals means that mental health assessments have become easier to organise and logistically more effective.

Despite these benefits, one of the most important difficulties psychiatrists experience, even after integration, is getting access information held by social work colleagues, and this is mainly because the IT systems in use across services are still different. The partnership between health and social care went ahead in many areas before a system was developed which would allow all professional groups access to information. In many areas this is still the case, with health and social care colleagues employed by the same organisation, and working in the same teams, yet having to input information into different data systems. This is a result of targets and indicators which demand that health and social care activity data is collected and 'fed' to different regulatory bodies. In many areas one IT system is yet to be established that can feed the various requirements of different inspection bodies, and members of the same team are thus unable to access each other's information records, which can lead to clinical difficulties, risks and frustrations.

Summary: integration or disintegration?

The general consensus among the psychiatric community within the area surveyed was one of positive regard towards the integration of health and social care. There remain a number of concerns and barriers towards full multi-disciplinary acceptance, but these concerns are expressed across the professional groups and are not specific to medical clinicians.

Issues such as shifting the balance of power, the definition of professional roles, bureaucratic management methods and cultural expectations are all areas that affect a profession's engagement with the change process, and medical professionals are not unique in their concerns and questions.

There were some areas of encouraging enthusiasm and respect between doctors and social workers. For example, some colleagues suggested increased involvement of social workers in the training of doctors. This is a potential future development, as although the undergraduate medical curriculum has clearly identified the role of social needs within the care of mental health service users, the involvement of social workers in the training of doctors has not yet been fully considered.

Integration may give medical colleagues an opportunity to involve social workers in the practical training of student doctors and trainees. This may involve such aspects as lectures from social workers, or attaching students to practising social workers for some time as part of their training, to get hands on experience of social work. Some colleagues also made suggestions such as joint assessments on a regular basis in accident and emergency and psychiatric wards with social workers, in order to promote holistic consideration of needs within all care environments.

Medical professionals are acutely aware of the models proposed in the *New Ways of Working* policy, and on the whole believe that integration of professions is a good idea; all disciplines are aiming to improve the patient's care, and because the medical consideration is by its nature centred around the health aspects, it is beneficial to have an alternative perspective contributing to the treatment planning process.

What is important within the integration process is that each profession learns from the other's expertise, and takes advantage of the other's training. By doing this the perspective that is brought to the care process is broadened. Unfortunately for many of the medical practitioners surveyed, the experience they have of their social work colleges is that they tend to focus their practice purely on social needs. As one psychiatrist commented:

> Nurses and doctors tend to have a broader recognition of the role of psychosocial needs on top of medical needs, but it appears to me social workers are keeping their practice focused on social work. (Staff grade psychiatrist)

With this being the case, social workers are at times viewed as inflexible in their approach, and as having little regard for the medical model of care. It is possible to consider needs from both a medical and social perspective, and some of the more traditional social work colleagues can be viewed as devaluing the medical perspective, a situation which is not conducive to partnership working.

While learning from other disciplines is an important aspect of continuing professional development, one final consideration in this discussion is the belief that workers need to maintain recognition of the limitations of their own training and practice. The definition and development of multi-disciplinary team working does not mean that everybody has equal skills, knowledge, training or authority. The power imbalance between professionals and the hierarchical systems that operate within the health service have had an impact upon the effectiveness of integration, and from a medical perspective the vying for control between the professions is both unhelpful and unwarranted.

A good number of psychiatrists, especially juniors and trainees, have very little idea about the partnership arrangements between health and social care within mental health service provision. Many did not see any difference between practice pre- and post-integration and this is indicative of the rapid changes and shifts in direction to which the NHS is subject. The lack of consultation with medical staff is a contributing factor to this phenomenon.

> We are not consulted prior to the change, the changes are not piloted or researched and once implemented we are told this is going to be a success story. (Consultant psychiatrist).

With this type of experience there is little wonder that clinicians choose to concentrate on their day-to-day practice, rather than on the climate of service provision and policy drivers.

The views of doctors about partnership working have generally been mixed, but mostly positive. There appears to be some element of lack of awareness or interest among some clinicians, and a view that the integration of services has made little difference to practice on the ground.

Despite these experiences and attitudes the majority of medical professionals surveyed did recognise the contribution of social work to the holistic assessment and treatment of needs.

Overall the aim of these changes is reviewed positively and as a step towards better patient care, the issues that medical colleagues have highlighted are largely in relation to how these changes are being managed and implemented within services.

Conclusion

This chapter has highlighted the issue that integration of services is not just an issue for social care, but that the other disciplines are also involved and experiencing the influence of joined-up provision.

Overall the medical perspective views the integration of services as a positive step and places value on the contribution that social work can make to the care of individuals with mental health problems.

Reflection point

What are your views of the comments and criticisms raised by medical colleagues? How will these views affect your practice?

Some of the comments made by medical colleagues can be challenging to hear from the social work perspective; however, recognition of the social work profession's engagement within the integration process is important if development and service improvement are to be achieved. It is often easy for social care to feel that it is being subsumed into health per-spectives without considering the role that professionals can play in this process, and differ-ing perspectives are therefore considered essential in the debate regarding the potential successes and failures of integrated care.

Further reading

Royal College of Psychiatry, Care Services Improvement Partnership and Social Care Institute for Excellence (2007). *A Common Purpose: Recovery in Future Mental Health Services*. RCP/CSIP/SCIE Joint Position Paper.

Chapter 12

The experience of substance misuse: a word from the voluntary sector

By Terry Bogg, Director of Services in a voluntary sector agency

Wisdom too often never comes, and so one ought not to reject it merely because it comes late. (Felix Frankfurter, American jurist, 1882–1965)

PQ framework

Achieving Post-qualifying Social Work awards

This chapter will assist in the meeting of National Occupational Standards for Social Work:

Key Role 5, Unit 17: Work within multi-disciplinary and multi-organisational teams, networks and systems.

Key Role 6, Unit 20: Manage complex ethical issues, dilemmas and conflicts.

For registered social workers considering, or working towards, post-qualifying awards, this chapter will also assist in meeting the requirements of both the specialist award in mental health and the national occupational standards in mental health, which are core to the post-qualification standards in this area.

MHNOS 57: Monitor, evaluate and improve processes for delivering mental health services to a population.

MHNOS 80: Explore, initiate and improve processes for developing collaborative working relationships.

PQ Specialist Award in Mental Health

47 (vii) Working collaboratively with other professions.

47 (x) Utilising appropriate knowledge and research from other disciplines.

Foreword by Daisy Bogg

The integration of health and social care is an agenda that is driving more than just the statutory providers of care. The independent, voluntary and private sectors provide an extensive amount of front line services, and are the agencies that health and social care commissioners look to in terms of creative use of resources and responsiveness to the service user groups.

Substance misuse, while being part of mental health services, is often treated as an alien issue and service, and the tendency for a lack of communication, coordination and cohesiveness between mental health and substance misuse provision is prevalent despite research evidence which states that the two issues are interlinked. The prevalence of so-called 'dual diagnosis' within both service user groups is extensive.

This chapter is a perspective provided by a professional working within the substance misuse service sector for a voluntary sector provider which is commissioned by the local Drug and Alcohol Action Team (DAAT) to provide a range of services within the community. The integration agenda is one that is reaching out across all areas of provision, and it is therefore necessary for health and social care professionals working within the statutory sector to develop an awareness and insight into how third-sector partners are experiencing these developments.

A voluntary sector perspective: the experience of substance misuse

'I'm sick, sir' was the reply given recently by a heroin user in court for shoplifting, when asked why he continually stole from local shops. This was his forty-second offence in three years.

'What's wrong with you?' his solicitor asked. 'I suffer from acute criminal behaviour' was the ironic but insightful response from a man who had seen his treatment needs remain constant for 12 years, but seen them met in a variety of ways by a variety of services, with the single consistency of failure.

The outcome? He was sentenced to a community-based drug rehabilitation requirement (DRR), predecessor of the drug treatment and testing orders (DTTO), and a programme that had spectacularly failed for him on at least two previous occasions.

You may ask why a service user, so seemingly entrenched in his using and criminal behaviour, should stand as an example of the failure of services. Surely it is the lack of motivation that sits at the hub of the problem? In a way you would be correct; certainly in current service provision only motivation of heroic proportions will lead you through the morass. Only the most determined will rise above the quagmire, stuck in services where contingency management is the norm and harm reduction is the buzzword. Never have the words 'be careful what you wish for, because that's the maximum you will receive' been more apt.

It is very difficult to give a national perspective on substance misuse services because there is no consistent delivery, with each DAAT able to commission services as it sees fit, as long as it meets targets laid down by the National Treatment Agency (NTA). Drug treatment is more of a postcode lottery than any other health-based treatment in England and Wales today. Of course this is where the paradox hits, because if you commit an acquisitive crime, or are found in possession of any illicit drug, and live in a Drug Intervention Programme (DIP) intensive area, then all your rights around health care treatment are ignored, your right to confidentiality is suspended, and the coercive right of Criminal Justice Intervention Team (CJIT) partnerships is brought to bear. For the service users, 'voluntary motivated engagement' becomes 'you will or else'.

It would not be right to suggest that all is wrong with DIP interventions; much that is good have come from them – Single Point of Contact (SPOC) and rapid entry into substitute prescribing to name but two. To some extent this is the area where integrated services perhaps work best, but it is the flawed reasoning behind it, and its effect on mainstream generic funding and therefore delivery, that sits at the heart of the problem.

The move to integrate health and social care within substance misuse services has tried to follow that of mental health and social care, but interestingly has in almost all cases been prevented from properly joining up with these services to offer a cohesive and holistic service.

For the most part, substance misuse services operate in silos, each with separate, and often competing, agendas and philosophies. Clinical pathways, where present, are often blurred, and the exchange of information is patchy at best. The services are staffed in the main by committed and trained individuals, and it is the lack of clear, concise, care planning, hindered by entrenched practice, that lies at the root of the problem. Often clients will be taken through endless assessments, as each participating agency reinforces its own particular part of the process, paying little or no regard to the information-gathering expertise of partners. With each agency working out of separate buildings, for the most part just getting through to a modality start can be an arduous process.

Taking an average sized county, with a mix of urban and rural areas, similar to my own, treatment may look as follows:

Using the Glasgow formula – 3,000 chaotic drug users (CDU) give or take 5 per cent:

- 1,300 in specialist prescribing services;

- 400 in shared care;

- 450 in tier 3 psychosocial treatment.

This leaves at least 1,000 individuals accessing tier 2, needle exchanges, or no services whatsoever. With a large and diverse black and minority ethnic (BME) population and the well-documented problems inherent in engaging with these groups, these numbers, while not perfect, are moving towards an acceptable estimation of the situation. This would suggest that the basic infrastructure of services is in place, but in reality it is a very different story.

As with many services, the non-statutory agency acts as gatekeeper to the statutory specialist service, and is the access point to tiers 3 and 4, while delivering tier 2 open-access and tier 3 psychosocial provisions, along with a range of specialist interventions, such as complex needs, children and families, and alternative therapies both alone and in partnership. Funded by the DAAT in one area to the tune of £750,000 annually, from a budget of £5.5 million, every client accessing any service within non-CJIT delivery must come via triage and assessment within them. Working very closely to the NTA target of three weeks from referral to first modality start, over 95 per cent of clients fit within this criterion. The problem is only obvious when you are made aware that over 60 per cent of all new clients to the service in the past year have been alcohol clients, where no such targets exist, and where funding for alcohol work sits at just 10 per cent of the overall agency budget.

Alcohol-dependent clients have no access to CJIT services pre-sentence at all, and only limited access post-sentence. This huge discrepancy between drug and alcohol provision has led to a dilution and contamination of services, as all services, statutory and non-statutory, try to 'keep the cork in the bottle' and offer a semblance of an effective service, and often fail.

Endless meetings take place, with endless declarations of intent, but in reality it all comes down to the same thing – 'nothing changes because nothing changes' – with each organisation looking to protect its part in the delivery structure in order to maintain, in certain cases, its very existence. As always in these situations it is the service user who suffers. The question always remains the same – how do we do it better?

I believe it can be done, but it involves some real risk-taking by the agencies concerned. With a limited budget, decreasing in real terms year on year, what we must do as a starting point is to map out all existing health and social care provision. We must understand who does what, where and with whom, and we must not seek to replicate already existing services. Having this information to hand, what comes next? This is probably the most important question we need to ask ourselves: what do we want substance misuse services to look like? When we know that, it is possible to consider how to adapt and change existing services and provisions.

To enable change to happen, we need a fundamental shift in the commissioning and procurement processes. All current service providers should be consulted individually and together. This collective expertise and experience would bring much added value to the table; however, this is also where the risk comes in, because the outcome of this practice may be anything from contracts being put out to tender, down to complete decommissioning, and many organisations are unwilling to take the risk.

Let's image that the outcome of this process is that all services are to be decommissioned, not to replace like with like, which has so often been the case (if nothing changes, nothing changes), but in order to offer a real alternative to current thinking.

I advocate the formation of social enterprise organisations, formed from identified and willing partners, who would deliver the whole package, using the Alternative Provider of Services (APS) model, so beloved by GP practice-based commissioning. This would enable agencies to come together within one new organisation – true integration. Using this model, there would be no duplication of roles, either clinical or administrative (I can hear all the third-party concerns cheering), and given the relentless eroding of full-cost recovery, free up even more resources.

Instead of agencies operating with a range of strategic plans, often in conflict with one another, the formation of a robust business model would drive the service forward. Controlling the entire budget, instead of individual silos of resource, accountability is coupled with responsibility, creating a vibrant organisation whose success is in its own hands rather than being dependent upon others, without the ability to influence, as is currently the case.

Having previously mapped existing health and social care services, well functioning clinical pathways can be negotiated with other services, such as the CMHT and general health care providers, with an overall target being to provide specialist supported care given by GPs but with the provision to refer into local centres for support.

Any centralised specialist service would be scaled down dramatically, and would work peripatetically, brought in as required but not holding a caseload. Care management in this scenario would remain within the APS. This model would not allow for any distinction between drug and alcohol clients, as the substance would be viewed as a symptom and not the cause of the problem.

If done properly and cost effectively, any surplus on the budget could be re-invested in service delivery. This of course would be dependent upon funding not being reduced every year by the amount of any surplus – over to you, government of the day! Given the amount of revenue successive governments have taken from the alcohol industry, is this too much to ask? There would of course be much work required in terms of workforce formation and the attainment of shared goals and values, but this is for the consideration of others more skilled than me. However, if we do ever find the courage to change our thinking and our practices, I believe that we will find the answer is in there somewhere.

I started with CJIT, and I would like to end there. For the most part custody workers see the same faces going round and round the system, a sensationally small number using a disproportionate amount of resources. The current thinking that all offenders who use drugs commit drug-driven crime is ludicrous in the extreme, and yet has driven our CJIT agenda over the last two years, costing millions upon millions of pounds.

There are some fantastic CJIT teams up and down the country – I know, I have one – and some boundary shifting work is being done in prisons – I know, because I worked in one. The problem is that for the most part, those who need prison-based services rarely get a sentence long enough for them to access them. Counselling, Assessment, Referral, Aftercare and Through care (CARAT) teams are subject to the same criteria as most prison-delivered services, 'my nick, my rules' being the noise most governors make. There are exceptions – you know who you are!

In reality it seems that we are trying to force into treatment the group of individuals whom most major studies (see Gossop et al., 2001 and NIAAA, 1996) say will never access services. Instead of spending untold millions on a small percentage of people at the point of arrest, why not invest in more programme spaces and staff, and put the money into housing and aftercare for those coming out of prisons – the two biggest indicators of recidivism in this country?

Conclusion

It appears from this narrative that similar issues to those experienced by statutory sector providers are being repeated within the voluntary and independent sector. Emphasis on integration and targets, along with the tendency for interested parties to adhere to their own interests and agendas, are common to us all: have we therefore achieved a state of consistent inconsistency within service delivery?

A different model of service provision is described within this chapter, one which appears to meet the needs of the integration agenda as well as the users of the services; however, as the author rightly asks, do providers and commissioners alike have the courage of their convictions? Can organisational cultures be shifted to such an extent that thinking can change and a new way forward within the sector be achieved? Many questions remain unanswered; however, it is possible to suggest from the experience detailed here that many of the challenges facing health and social care providers are also being experienced within the substance misuse sector and by non-statutory providers of care.

Further reading

National Treatment Agency (2008) *Non Medical Prescribing, Patient Group Directions, and Minor Ailment Schemes in the Treatment of Drug Misusers*. Available at www.nta.nhs.uk

NICE (2007) *Drug Misuse and Dependence: Clinical Guidelines on Drug Misuse and Dependence*. London: Department of Health.

NICE (2007) *Compact Guidance on Commissioning Voluntary Sector Services*. London: Department of Health.

Chapter 13

The integration agenda: what have we learnt so far?

Learning without thought is labour lost; thought without learning is perilous.
Confucius (551 BC–479 BC)

PQ framework

Achieving Post-qualifying Social Work awards

This chapter will assist in the meeting of National Occupational Standards for Social Work:

Key Role 5, Unit 15: Contribute to the management of resources and services.
Key Role 6, Unit 18: Research, analyse, evaluate and use current knowledge of best social work practice.
Key Role 6, Unit 19: Work within agreed standards of social work practice and ensure own professional development.

For registered social workers considering, or working towards, post-qualifying awards, this chapter will also assist in meeting the requirements of both the specialist award in mental health and the national occupational standards in mental health, which are core to the post-qualification standards in this area.

MHNOS 81: Sustain and review collaborative working.
MHNOS 86: Monitor, evaluate and improve inter-agency services for addressing mental health needs.

PQ Specialist Award in Mental Health

47 (iv) The legal and policy context of mental health including awareness of relevant local, as well as national, policy contexts.
47 (x) Utilising appropriate knowledge and research from other disciplines including relevant research from people who use services and carers, and contributing to the generation and promotion of evidence-based practice through the application or conduct of research in mental health social work.

Introduction

This book has discussed a range of issues concerning the integration of health and social care services. Mental health care in England and Wales has seen significant development over the past ten years, with a range of initiatives all designed to assist with the delivery of the NSF and improve the quality of care services.

The differences between health care and social care have been the subject of a range of debates. It is difficult to define clearly the boundaries between the two areas, but the fact remains that they operate within different perspectives and cultures, and have differing agendas in terms of the delivery of services. Despite these differences the government agenda has retained clarity of purpose, with the aim of joining up and integrating the two areas of provision. This direction has infiltrated all the policy and good practice guidelines within the field over the previous decade.

The previous chapters have detailed areas such as professional perspectives, different models of delivery, staff experiences and what the integration agenda means to the users of services. This final chapter attempts to draw all these strands together and to highlight the key areas of learning.

Integration has been on the agenda for nearly a decade, with varying levels of success reported across the country. It is now time to step back from the process of change, and to enable a period of reflection, asking what we have learnt from the experience so far.

Professionalism and integration

There has been significant discussion over the past decade regarding the social work profession and where it fits into the integration agenda. Chapters 4 and 5 contributed to this discussion, considering the range of developments that have occurred as a result of the modernisation agenda from the social care perspective.

Professionalism is an issue that social workers have been debating, and striving for recognition of, for many years. However, it was not until relatively recently, with the inception of the GSCC (as a result of the Care Standards Act 2000), that professional registration and protection of title were introduced. This development occurred at the same time as the formation of partnership trusts, when many social workers found themselves either employed by the NHS, or operating within health care teams. This represented a significant perceived threat to social workers across the country, and many organisations, including BASW, expressed concerns regarding the integrity and independence of the social work role (particularly in regard to the ASW functions). The NHS culture and medical model approach was seen as in direct opposition to the social work value base and functions, and as a result many workers felt that the change in organisational emphasis would undermine their ability to maintain their professional identity.

Despite these concerns, the integration of services remains the strategic vision in terms of improving services. Professional concerns were originally expressed in a range of forums; however, these now appear to be subsiding, with recognition that the drivers for modernisation are consistent, and ultimately in the best interests of those who use the services.

The concept of professionalism is difficult to define in concrete terms, but there are some common characteristics that are applicable to all professional groups. These include technical skill, codes of ethical conduct, application of theoretical knowledge appropriate to discipline, identification with the given profession, and appropriate standards of behaviour. The employment environment in which the professional operates is not part of the concept, and should therefore not be relevant in terms of identity. However, as discussed elsewhere in this book, this is actually not the case, and the nature of the employer has been the cause of significant concern among professional groups. For social workers within the health service, the task should be to remain committed to the ideals of the value base on which the profession is founded, rather than to focus upon which organisation holds their terms and conditions of employment.

The integration agenda does not pose a significant threat to the social work profession; however, the process of change is something that is often unsettling. The person behind the professional seeks familiarity as a means of retaining a sense of control over a given situation. With this in mind it could be suggested that the emphasis on the employer, as a part of the professional identity, is a way of retaining a link to the known, as opposed to any actual or tangible impact upon the role that results from working within the NHS environment.

This discussion does not seek to dismiss the concerns that social work and social care professionals have regarding working in a health environment. It does, however, suggest that the threat to the profession may be perceived rather than actual. This is especially the case when considering the recent developments regarding capability frameworks, which have a value-based approach that is wholly consistent with the social care perspective.

Policy and integration

As discussed in the early chapters of this book, the policy direction of the integration of health and social care has remained consistent over the last decade. Both policy and legislation, contributing to the modernisation of services across the sector, have seen a range of developments in terms not only of how disciplines operate but also of the way services are provided.

Full integration of provision has not yet been achieved, and in some areas health and social care organisations have merged, and then subsequently been dissolved, due to failing performance or the perceived inability of agencies to deliver the agenda of their partners. Reviews, such as that reported on by Dame Denise Platt (2006), have reinforced the questions regarding whether the NHS is best placed to deliver social care. This has been further compounded by the discrepancies in some of the funding and access criteria, which have created significant challenges.

It is clear from the range of policy that has been issued, encompassing competency, practice, organisation and governance arrangements, that the integration agenda remains high on the government agenda, and agencies will be required to demonstrate their continued ability to deliver on this agenda if they are to survive within the health and social care economy.

Partnership models and integration

A number of models and concepts of partnership have been discussed throughout this text, and questions have been raised regarding whether partnership between health and social care organisations is possible. There are clearly both benefits and adverse consequences associated with integrative models, and no absolute conclusion regarding the best approach has been reached. Despite this there are a number of key conclusions with regard to good practice in partnerships that can be applied. These are:

- **Clarity of roles and responsibilities**: Staff within multi-disciplinary and partnership environments need to be aware of not only their own roles and responsibilities, but also those of their colleagues and partners. This is equally important across the different management tiers – from front line service delivery to strategic committees.

- **Clarity of rationale for change**: All the stakeholders involved in the change environment need to be aware of why it is occurring. This promotes engagement and buy-in throughout the organisation.

- **Development of shared goals, vision and agenda**: Along with clarity of rationale, stakeholders need purpose and direction to encourage success in partnership arrangements. Competing and conflicting goals and agendas are not conducive to partnership, and consistent leadership is required to drive the process.

- **The ability to measure success and/or failure objectively**: In order to sustain partnership and maintain roles and responsibility, there is a need to apply key performance indicators and objective measurement standards. Without these frameworks partners have the potential to shift responsibility without a clear route of redress.

- **Skill mix and valuing multi-disciplinary approaches**: For multi-disciplinary working to be successful the disciplines involved need to develop a mutual respect and understanding of each other's skills and perspectives.

- **Identification of, and consultation, with stakeholders**: Organisations and partnership arrangements are often very internal looking, and it is necessary for public sector providers to consider other stakeholders. These may include service users, carers and voluntary sector providers, all of whom have the potential to influence the overall success of partnership arrangements.

- **Consideration of people and culture, as well as process**: The human elements involved in organisations cannot be ignored, and while process is an important factor it should not be the sole focus.

Reorganisation for reorganisation's sake is one of the criticisms that is often levelled at statutory sector organisations, and one which is often unwarranted. However, if agencies do not share the rationale with staff and service users, these groups will become increasingly sceptical and cynical when change is proposed.

> **Reflection point**
>
> How easy is it to identify the partnership good practice points in your working environments?
>
> To what extent are staff consulted and involved in reorganisations within your agency?

The communication between organisations and their stakeholders is a key area that requires attention, whether this is with other agencies, service users or staff teams. Those involved need to feel listened to and considered within the process, and able to share the front line experience of the implications of integration initiatives.

Linking policy, partnership and the social work profession

Social work is a profession that is intrinsically linked to the socio-economic and political environments in which it operates. This means that the application of the given policy agenda is not a new phenomenon to either the profession, or those operating within it. Despite this familiarity with the concept of partnerships and systems within the wider social environment, social care staff have found the integrative process challenging.

Fragmentation of services is one of the main reasons for the integration agenda, but the process itself has created a degree of fragmentation, and the differences in local interpretation have had an impact upon this situation. It seems that as other professions have taken on board the recovery model, which is integral to the social perspective, those who should be at the forefront of the developments, that is social care staff, have increasingly withdrawn from the process. The reasons for this are multi-faceted, as has been discussed throughout this text, and issues such as the location of services within health organisations and a scarcity in the social care workforce (which is now being addressed) have contributed to the situation.

Considering the integration process from an objective standpoint, there is a clear linkage between policy and partnership processes, and the modernisation agenda has consistently applied the principle that the future of service delivery lies within a joined-up and seamless provision. This being the case, the social work profession is required to play a full part in the process if it is to influence the development of health and social care organisations and ensure that the profession remains both viable and valued within the integrated environment. *New Ways of Working* has the potential to assist in this task, with social work receiving equal attention to other disciplines, with emphasis upon leadership, research and evidence-based practice. These areas are intended to promote the social model within the modernisation debate, and enable social care to contribute fully to the developmental plans.

> **Reflection point**
>
> How would you encourage social work colleagues within your area to contribute to the development and improvement of mental health services?

Integration – ten years on

After ten years of developments and service improvement initiatives designed to promote the integration of health and social care, it is prudent to consider the progress that has been made so far, and evaluate what has been learnt from the experiences.

The previous chapters of this book have considered integration from a range of perspectives, throughout which one message has been clear: although the improvement of service user access and the increase in treatment effectiveness are universally considered to be positive steps, the delivery of these aims has been somewhat variable. Differences in approach, attitude and agenda have given rise to a range of challenges for those working within the services, and partners within the process have experienced a range of difficulties in terms of developing objective measurements and shared goals for the delivery of services.

As public sector organisations continue to develop and deliver services, there is a tendency to react rather than plan ahead. This response is often driven by political and economic factors, with increasing pressure being exerted at all levels of organisations. Inquiries, such as those arising from suicide and homicide incidents, are a clear example of these pressures. There is a tendency, when considering mental health-related incidents, to focus on the responsibilities of the organisations to the exclusion of all other stakeholders. While this level of scrutiny is required in terms of delivering transparent and accountable services, there is also a need to consider the human element, and the professionals tasked to deliver these services, who can be as unsure and fallible as other members of society.

What have we learnt?

In terms of the learning that can be derived from the experience of integration so far, the following points need to be considered. This is not a definitive list, but rather an indication of some of the areas from which learning can be developed and applied.

1. Organisations need to be considered within a whole-systems approach – with equal emphasis on the people as well as the process.

2. Partnerships are often difficult to manage – clarity of aims and clear evaluation mechanisms need to be in place from the outset.

3. Integration of health and social care is about more than structures – perspectives need to be aligned and compromises agreed to ensure all involved are 'singing from the same song sheet'.

4. Social care is often the 'poor cousin' in health care organisations, and all staff and

managers require training to ensure that they understand the frameworks and perspectives, prior to having responsibility for their delivery.

5. The model of integration is dependent upon local interpretation, and therefore needs to consider pre-existing and historical relationships.

6. The service user experience is intended to be the main focus of the integration agenda, yet the methods of measurement are often focused on quantity rather than quality. This is a situation that requires attention if the experience is to be improved in a tangible way.

7. Integration is not a threat to the social work profession; however, the perceived threat is creating a defensiveness and reluctance to engage among workers. There are many reasons why the response from social workers is not wholly positive, and these need to be explored both locally and nationally.

8. There are a range of good practice examples from integrated teams across the country, and while these appear in the policy documentation many practitioners are not aware of such developments. Managers and practitioners need to take ownership of their own service areas and it may be that local promotion of practice initiatives could contribute towards this aim.

9. In terms of the hierarchy of health organisations, social care staff are often under-represented at both ground and higher levels, with a lack of strong social care leadership throughout NHS Trusts. Investment in people is required to address this situation, and leadership development programmes, in which social care staff are encouraged to participate, may be beneficial in terms of creating future leaders within the sector.

10. Social workers need to recognise that many of the developments within the field, such as competency frameworks and recovery driven approaches, are based upon social perspectives, and an overall acknowledgement of the contribution of social care from health employers, on a local level, may assist in this aim.

Many other points and considerations have arisen in the course of this book, and no claims are made here to provide any definitive answers. The aim throughout this book has been to consider the impact of integration from a social work perspective, and as a consequence the implications for health colleagues have received little attention.

The developments within the mental health services in this country are dynamic and in a state of flux, and while learning points can be identified, a significant amount of work is still required before the ideal of 'seamless' services is achieved.

This chapter opened with a quote from Confucius stating that learning and thought were integral to each other. This book has reinforced this linkage throughout. Often the journey is more important than the destination, and for the social work profession it is vital that learning and reflection from the integrative experience are incorporated into both the evidence base and the practice, since traditionally this is how the social care perspective has developed. By embracing this reflection, rather than seeing integration as a threat to the profession, it can be viewed as an opportunity from which social work as a professional approach can grow.

More questions than answers?

As a final point, readers are left to consider and reflect upon the following issues for inclusion into both their practice and their future development:

- How can the social work profession be empowered to use its collective voice?

- How can new workers be encouraged to practice within the health environment?

- How can full representation and inclusion of service user views be incorporated?

- How can partnership relationships be objectively measured?

- How can the experience of voluntary sector organisations be utilised?

- Can inter-professional training be used to promote integration within services?

- How can professional and organisational cultures be adapted and developed?

- How can integration, as an approach, be better managed within organisations?

Appendix 1

Principles of BASW Code of Ethics

Social work is committed to five basic values:

1. Human dignity and worth
2. Social justice
3. Service to humanity
4. Integrity
5. Competence.

Social work practice should both promote respect for human dignity and pursue social justice. (BASW, 1977)

Appendix 2

National Occupational Standards for Social Work – key roles

(TOPSS (2001) NOS Social Work)

Key role 1

Prepare for, and work with individuals, families, carers, groups and communities to assess their needs and circumstances.

Key role 2

Plan, carry out, review and evaluate social work practice, with individuals, families, carers, groups, communities and other professionals.

Key role 3

Support individuals to represent their needs, views and circumstances.

Key role 4

Manage risk to individuals, families, carers, groups, communities, self and colleagues.

Key role 5

Manage and be accountable for, with supervision and support, your own social work practice within your organisation.

Key role 6

Demonstrate professional competence in social work practice.

Appendix 3

GSCC (2002) Code of Conduct for Social Care Employees

1 As a social care worker, you must protect the rights and promote the interests of service users and carers. This includes:

1.1 treating each person as an individual;

1.2 respecting and, where appropriate, promoting the individual views and wishes of both service users and carers;

1.3 supporting service users' rights to control their lives and make informed choices about the services they receive;

1.4 respecting and maintaining the dignity and privacy of service users;

1.5 promoting equal opportunities for service users and carers; and

1.6 respecting diversity and different cultures and values.

2 As a social care worker, you must strive to establish and maintain the trust and confidence of service users and carers. This includes:

2.1 being honest and trustworthy;

2.2 communicating in an appropriate, open, accurate and straightforward way;

2.3 respecting confidential information and clearly explaining agency policies about confidentiality to service users and carers;

2.4 being reliable and dependable;

2.5 honouring work commitments, agreements and arrangements and, when it is not possible to do so, explaining why to service users and carers;

2.6 declaring issues that might create conflicts of interest and making sure that they do not influence your judgement or practice; and

2.7 adhering to policies and procedures about accepting gifts and money from service users and carers.

3 As a social care worker, you must promote the independence of service users while protecting them as far as possible from danger or harm. This includes:

3.1 promoting the independence of service users and assisting them to understand and exercise their rights;

3.2 using established processes and procedures to challenge and report dangerous, abusive, discriminatory or exploitative behaviour and practice;

3.3 following practice and procedures designed to keep you and other people safe from violent and abusive behaviour at work;

3.2 bringing to the attention of your employer or the appropriate authority resource or operational difficulties that might get in the way of the delivery of safe care;

3.3 informing your employer or an appropriate authority where the practice of colleagues may be unsafe or adversely affecting standards of care;

3.4 complying with employers' health and safety policies, including those relating to substance abuse;

3.5 helping service users and carers to make complaints, taking complaints seriously and responding to them or passing them to the appropriate person; and

3.8 recognising and using responsibly the power that comes from your work with service users and carers.

4 As a social care worker, you must respect the rights of service users while seeking to ensure that their behaviour does not harm themselves or other people. This includes:

4.1 recognising that service users have the right to take risks and helping them to identify and manage potential and actual risks to themselves and others;

4.2 following risk assessment policies and procedures to assess whether the behaviour of service users presents a risk of harm to themselves or others;

4.3 taking necessary steps to minimise the risks of service users from doing actual or potential harm to themselves or other people; and

4.4 ensuring that relevant colleagues and agencies are informed about the outcomes and implications of risk assessments.

5 As a social care worker, you must uphold public trust and confidence in social care services. In particular you must not:

5.1 abuse, neglect or harm service users, carers or colleagues;

5.2 exploit service users, carers or colleagues in any way;

5.3 abuse the trust of service users and carers or the access you have to personal information about them or to their property, home or workplace;

5.4 form inappropriate personal relationships with service users;

5.5 discriminate unlawfully or unjustifiably against service users, carers or colleagues;

5.6 condone any unlawful or unjustifiable discrimination by service users, carers or colleagues;

5.7 put yourself or other people at unnecessary risk; or

5.8 behave in a way, in work or outside work, which would call into question your suitability to work in social care services.

6 As a social care worker, you must be accountable for the quality of your work and take responsibility for maintaining and improving your knowledge and skills. This includes:

6.1 meeting relevant standards of practice and working in a lawful, safe and effective way;

6.2 maintaining clear and accurate records as required by procedures established for your work;

6.3 informing your employer or the appropriate authority about any personal difficulties that might affect your ability to do your job competently and safely;

6.4 seeking assistance from your employer or the appropriate authority if you do not feel able or adequately prepared to carry out any aspect of your work, or you are not sure about how to proceed in a work matter;

6.5 working openly and cooperatively with colleagues and treating them with respect;

6.6 recognising that you remain responsible for the work that you have delegated to other workers;

6.7 recognising and respecting the roles and expertise of workers from other agencies and working in partnership with them; and

6.8 undertaking relevant training to maintain and improve your knowledge and skills and contributing to the learning and development of others.

Bibliography

Publications

Age Concern (2007) New continuing care figures show unfairness of system. Available at: http://www.ageconcern.org.uk

Allott, P., Loganathan, L. and Fulford, K. W. M. (2002) Discovering hope for recovery. *Canadian Journal of Community Mental Health*, 21(2), 13–34.

American Psychiatric Association (2000) (4th edn) *Diagnostic and Statistical Manual of Mental Disorders DSM-IV-TR*. Washington: American Psychiatric Association.

Anderson, N. R. and West, M. A. (1998) Measuring climate for work group innovation: development and validation of the team climate inventory. *Journal of Organizational Behavior*, 19 (3), 235–58.

Andreoli, A. (1997) The quality of the human context as a factor in treatment. *Therapeutic Communities*, 18 (1), 15–26.

Anthony, W. A. (1993) Recovery from mental illness: The guiding vision of the mental health service system in the 1990s. *Psychosocial Rehabilitation Journal*, 16 (4), 11–23.

Appleby, L. (2004) *The National Service Framework for Mental Health – Five Years On*. London: DoH, TSO.

Audit Commission (2005) *Governing Partnerships: Bridging the Accountability Gap*. London: TSO.

Association of Directors of Social Services (2006) *Survey of Approved Social Workers in England*. London: ADSS.

Bagnall, A-M., Jones, L., Ginnelly, L., Lewis, R., Glanville, J., Gilbody, S., Davies, L., Torgerson, D. and Kleijnen, J. (2003) A systematic review of atypical antipsychotic drugs in schizophrenia. *Health Technology Assessment*, 7 (13), 1–193.

Balloch, S. and Taylor, M. (Eds) (2001) *Partnership Working: Policy and Practice*. Bristol: The Policy Press.

Banks, S. (1998) Professional ethics in social work – what future? *British Journal of Social Work*, 28 (2), 213–31.

Barnes, M. and Shardlow, P. (1997) From passive recipient to active citizen: participation in mental health user groups. *Journal of Mental Health*, 6 (3), 289–300.

Bartz, R. (1999) Beyond the biopsychosocial model new approaches to doctor-patient interactions. *The Journal of Family Practice*, 48 (8), 339–40. Available at: http://findarticles.com/p/articles/mi_m0689/is_8_48/ai_59407902.

BASW (1977) *Code of Ethics for Social Workers*. Birmingham: BASW.

Bedfordshire and Hertfordshire Strategic Health Authority (2003) *Continuing Care Criteria for Adults aged 18 and over in*

Bibliography

Bedfordshire and Hertfordshire. Available at: http://www.bhha.nhs.uk/publications/docs/ continuingcarecriteriawithamendments.pdf

Bentall, R. (2004) *Madness Explained: Psychosis and Human Nature*. London: Penguin.

Berrios, G. E. and Hauser, R. (1988) The early developments of Kraeplin's ideas on classification: a conceptual history. *Psychological Medicine*, 18, 813–21.

Bogg, D. (2007) An injection of social care. *Community* Care, 29/03/07, 31.

Bradshaw, M. (2002) Social work with older persons. In Jacoby, R. and Oppenheimer, C. (Eds) *Psychiatry in the Elderly*. Oxford: Oxford University Press.

Brown, A. and Bourne, I. (1995) *Social Work Supervisor: Supervision in Community, Day Care, and Residential Settings (Supervision in Context)*. Buckingham: Open University Press.

Brown, G. W. and Harris, T. (1978). *Social Origins of Depression. A Study of Psychiatric Disorder in Women*. London: Tavistock.

Brown, H. and Smith, H. (1989) Whose 'ordinary life' is it anyway? *Disability and Society*, 4 (2), 105–19

Bruce, M., Takeuchi, D. and Leaf, P. (1991) Poverty and psychiatric status: longitudinal evidence from the New Haven epidemiologic catchment area study. *Archives of General Psychiatry*, 48 (5), 470–74.

Buck, P. W and. Alexander, L. B. (2006) Neglected voices: consumers with serious mental illness speak about intensive case management. *Administration and Policy in Mental Health and Mental Health Services Research*, 33 (4), 470.

Byrne. P. (2000) Stigma of mental illness and ways of diminishing it. *Advances in Psychiatric Treatment*, 6, 62.

Carey, M. (2003) Anatomy of a care manager. *Work, Employment and Society*, 17 (1), 1235.

Cambridge, P., Forrester-Jones, R., Carpenter, J., Tate, A., Knapp, M., Beecham, J. and Hallam, A. (2005) The state of care management in learning disability and mental health services 12 years into community care. *British Journal of Social Work*, 35 (7), 1030–62.

Challis, D. and Ferlie, E. (1987) Changing patterns of fieldwork: organization: II: the team leaders' view. *British Journal of Social Work*, 17 (15), 1467.

Carpenter, J., Schneider, J., Brandon, T. and Wooff, D. (2003) Working in multidisciplinary community mental health teams: the impact on social workers and health professionals of integrated mental health care. *British Journal of Social Work*, 33 (8), 1081–9.

Carpenter, M. C. (2002) mental health recovery paradigm: implications for social work. *Health and Social Work*, 27 (2), 86–92.

Carpenter, M. C. and Platt, S. (1997) Professional identity for clinical social workers: impact of changes in health care delivery systems. *Clinical Social Work Journal*, 25 (3), 337–50.

CCETSW (1989; revised edn 1995) *Assuring Quality in the Diploma of Social Work*. London: CCETSW.

Cherniss, C. and Egnatios, E. (1978) Is there job satisfaction in community mental health? *Community Mental Health Journal*, 14 (4), 309–18.

CIPFA/SOLICE (2007) *Delivering Good Governance in Local Government*. London: CIPFA.

Commission for Social Care Inspection (2007a) *Performance Assessment Framework: Outcomes and Grade Descriptors*. London: CSCI.

Commission for Social Care Inspection (2007b) *Performance Assessment Framework 2007/8*. London: CSCI.

Commission for Social Care Inspection (2006) *Performance Ratings for Adult Social Services in England 2005/6*. London: CSCI.

Commission for Social Care Inspection (2004) *Performance Ratings for Adult Social Services in England 2003/4*. London: CSCI.

Commission for Social Care Inspection (2002) *Performance Ratings for Adult Social Services in England 2001/2*. London: CSCI.

Commission for Social Care Inspection (2000) *Performance Ratings for Adult Social Services in England 2000*. London: CSCI.

Community Care (2007) *New Continuing Care Rules May Spark Cash Row Between Councils and NHS*. 22/3/07. Available at: http://www.communitycare.co.uk

Cree, V. E. (2002) Social work and society. In Davies, M. (Ed.) *Blackwell Companion to Social Work* (2nd edn). Oxford: Blackwell.

CSIP (2008) *Creating Capable Teams*. London: Department of Health.

Currie, V., Harvy, G., West, E., McKenna, H. and Keeney, S. (2005) Relationship between quality of care, staffing levels, skill mix and nurse autonomy: literature review. *Journal of Advanced Nursing*, 51 (1), 73–82.

Dalley, G. (1991) Beliefs and behaviour: professionals and the policy process. *Journal of Aging Studies*, 5 (2), 163–80.

Davis, A. and Braithwaite, T. (2001) In our own hands. *Mental Health Care*, 41, 4114.

Deegan, P.E. (1988). Recovery: the lived experience of rehabilitation. *Psychosocial Rehabilitation Journal*, 11 (4), 19.

Department of Health (2008) *Transforming Social Care*. London: DH/TSO.

Department of Health (2007a) *Mental Health: New Ways of Working for Everyone*. London: TSO.

Department of Health (2007b) *National Framework for NHS Continuing Healthcare and NHS-funded Nursing Care in England*. London: TSO.

Department of Health (2007c) *Decision-Support Tool for NHS Continuing Healthcare: Version 2*. London: TSO.

Department of Health (2006) *Our Health, Our Care, Our Say*. London: TSO.

Department of Health (2005) *Independence, Well-being and Choice* London: TSO.

Department of Health (2004) *The Ten Essential Shared Capabilities: A Framework for the Whole of the Mental Health Workforce*. London: DoH.

Department of Health (2003) *Fair Access to Care Services: Guidance on Eligibility Criteria for Adult Social Care*. London: TSO.

Department of Health (2002) *Positive Approaches to the Integration of Health and Social Care in Mental Health Services*. London: TSO.

Department of Health (2000). *The NHS Plan: A Plan for Investment, a Plan for Reform*. London: TSO.

Department of Health (1999a) *Effective Care Co-ordination in Mental Health Service – Modernising the Care Programme Approach: A Policy Booklet*. London: TSO.

Department of Health (1999b) *National Service Framework for Mental Health: Modern Standards and Service Models* London: TSO.

Department of Health (1998a) *Modernising Mental Health Services: Safe, Sound and Supportive*. London: TSO.

Department of Health (1998b) *A First Class Service: Quality in the New NHS*. London: TSO.

Department of Health (1998c) *Modernising Social Services*. London: TSO.

Department of Health (1991) *The Care Programme Approach*. London: TSO.

Department of Health (1990) *Care Programme Approach*. London: TSO.

Desombre, T. and Eccles, G. (1998) Improving service quality in NHS Trust hospitals: lessons from the hotel sector. *International Journal of Health Care Quality Assurance*, 11 (1), 21–6.

DiMaggio, P. and Powell, W. W. (1991) *The New Institutionalism in Organizational Analysis*. Chicago: University of Chicago Press.

Dinsdale, P. (2006) Campaign for continuing care. *Nursing Older People*. 18 (4), 7–9.

Dix, A. (2004) Clinical management special: mental health – one to chew over. *Health Service Journal*, 1, (114), 28–9.

Double, D. (2002) Beyond biomedical models: a perspective from critical psychiatry. In Tew, J. (Ed.) *Social Perspectives in Mental Health*. London: Jessica Kingsley.

Double, D. B. (2000) Can psychiatry be retrieved from a biological approach? *Journal of Critical Psychology, Counselling and Psychotherapy*, 1 (1), 28–31.

Double, D. B. (1990) What would Adolf Meyer have thought of the neo-Kraepelinian approach? *Psychiatric Bulletin*, 14, 47.

Duggan, M. with Cooper, A. and Foster, J. (2002) *Modernising the Social Model in Mental Health: A Discussion Paper*. SPN Paper 1, London: SPN.

Edwards, D., Burnard, P., Coyle, D., Fothergill, A. and Hannigan, B. (2000) Stress and burnout in community mental health nursing: a review of the literature. *Journal of Psychiatric and Mental Health Nursing*, 7 (1), 4.

Ellis, K., Davis, A., and Rummery, K. (1999) Needs assessment, street-level bureaucracy and the new community care. *Social Policy and Administration*, 33 (3), 262–80.

Engel, G. (1980) The clinical application of the biopsychosocial model. *American Journal of Psychiatry*, 137, 5344.

Engel, G. (1977) The need for a new medical model: a challenge for biomedicine. *Science*, 8, 126.

Evans, S., Huxley, P., Webber, M., Katona, C., Gately, C., Mears, A., Medina, J., Pajak. and Kendall. T. (2005) The impact of statutory duties on mental health social workers in the UK. *Health and Social Care in the Community*, 13 (2), 145–54.

Fitzsimmons, P. and White, T. (1997) Crossing boundaries: communication between professional groups. *Journal of Management in Medicine*, 11 (2), 901.

Flood, R. L. (1999) *Rethinking the Fifth Discipline: Learning Within the Unknowable*. London: Routledge.

Frese, F.J., Stanley, J., Kress, K. and Vogel-Scibilia, S. (2001) Integrating evidence-based practices and the recovery model. *Psychiatric Services*, 52 (11), 1462–8.

Fulford, K. W. M. (2005) Values in Psychiatric Diagnosis: Developments in Policy, Training and Research *Psychopathology*, 38, 171–6.

Galatzer-Levy, I. R. and Galatzer-Levy, R. M. (2007) The revolution in psychiatric diagnosis: problems at the foundations. *Perspectives in Biology and Medicine*, 50 (2), 161–80.

Geddes, J., Freemantle, N., Harrison, P. and Bebbington, P. (2000) Atypical antipsychotics in the treatment of schizophrenia: systematic overview and meta-regression analysis. *British Medical Journal*, 321 (7273), 1371–6.

Gibb, C. E., Morrow, M., Clarke, C., Cook, G., Gertig, P. and Ramprogus, V. (2002) Trans-disciplinary working: evaluating the development of health and social care provision in mental health. *Journal of Mental Health*, 11 (3), 339–50.

Gilbert, P. (2003) *The Value of Everything: Social Work and Its Importance in the Field of Mental Health*. Lyme Regis: Russel House Publishing.

Gill, C (1994). *Two Models of Disability*. Chicago: University of Chicago.

Gladwell, M. (2000) *The Tipping Point: How Little Things Can Make a Big Difference*. Boston: Little, Brown.

Glasby, J. (2006) Bringing down the Berlin Wall: partnership working and the health and social care divide. *Health and Social Care in the Community*, 14 (3), 1996.

Glasby, J. and Peck, E. (2003) *Care Trusts: Partnership Working in Action*. Abingdon: Radcliffe.

Golightly, M. (2006) (2nd edn) *Mental Health and Social Work*. Exeter: Learning Matters.

Gossop, M., Marsden, J. and Stewart, D. (2001) *NTORS after Five Years (National Treatment Outcome Research Study): Changes in Substance Use, Health and Criminal Behaviour in the Five Years after Intake*. London: Department of Health.

Gröne, O. and Garcia-Barbero, M. (2001) Integrated care: a position paper of the WHO European Office for Integrated Health Care Services. *International Journal of Integrated Care*, 1 (1). Available at: www.ijic.org

GSCC (2007a) *Social Work: Roles and Tasks Consultation*. London: GSCC.

GSCC (2007b) *Specialist Standards for Post-Qualifying Social Work Education and Training: Social Work in Mental Health Services*. London: GSCC.

GSCC (2002) *Code of Conduct for Social Care Workers*. London: GSCC.

Hafford-Letchfield, T. (2006) *Practising Quality Assurance in Social Work*. Exeter: Learning Matters.

Harris, J. (2000) Is there a coherent social conception of disability? *Journal of Medical Ethics*, 26, 95–100.

Harvey, G. and Kitson, A. (1996) Achieving improvement through quality. *Journal of Advanced Nursing*, 24 (1), 185–95.

Health Care Commission (2007) *Survey of Users of Mental Health Services*. London: HCC.

Health Care Commission (2006a) *Survey of Users of Mental Health Services*. London: HCC.

Health Care Commission (2006b) *Standards for Better Health*. London: Department of Health.

Health Care Commission (2005) *Survey of Users of Mental Health Services*. London: HCC.

Health Care Commission (2004) *Survey of Users of Mental Health Services*. London: HCC.

Health Care Commission and Commission for Social Care Inspection (2007) *No Voice, No Choice: A joint review of adult community mental health services in England*. London: HCC.

Health Service Select Committee (2005) *Health – Sixth Report*. London: House of Commons.

Hewitt, J. (2005) Therapeutic working relationships with people with schizophrenia: literature review. *Journal of Advanced Nursing*, 52 (5), 561–70.

Higham, P. (2006) *Social Work: Introducing Professional Practice*. London: Sage.

Hodges, S., Nesman, T. and Hernandez, M. (1998) *Promising Practices: Building Collaboration in Systems of Care*. Systems of Care Promising Practices in Mental Health Series, vol. 6. Washington, DC: American Institutes for Research.

Hogg, M. A. and Abrams, D. (Eds) *Intergroup Relations: An Essential Reader*. Philadelphia: Psychology Press.

Holloway, F. (1991) Case management for the mentally ill: looking at the evidence. *International Journal of Social Psychiatry*, 37 (1), 2–13.

Howgego, I. M, Yellowlees, P., Owen, C., Meldrum, L. and Dark, F. (2003) The therapeutic alliance: the key to effective patient outcome? A descriptive review of the evidence in community mental health case management. *Australian and New Zealand Journal of Psychiatry*, 37 (2), 169–83.

Hudson, B. (2002) Interprofessionality in health and social care: the Achilles' heel of partnership? *Journal of Interprofessional Care*, 16 (1), 7–17.

Huxley, P., Evans, S., Webber, M. and Gately, C. (2005) Staff shortages in the mental health workforce: the case of the disappearing approved social worker. *Health and Social Care in the Community*, 13 (6), 504–13.

Huxley, P. and Kerfoot, C. (1994) A survey of approved social work in England and Wales. *British Journal of Social Work*, 24 (3), 311–24.

Iles, V. and Sutherland, K. (2006) *Managing Change in the NHS: Organisation Change, a Review for Health Care Managers, Professionals and Researchers*. London: NCC/SDO.

Illich, I. (1977) *Disabling Professions*. London: Marion Boyars.

Integrated Care Network and CSIP (2005) *Bringing the NHS and Local Government Together: Integrating the Workforce, A Guide*. London: ICN.

Integrated Care Network, CSIP and DoH (2006) *Practice Based Commissioning: An Introduction for a Local Authority Audience*. London: TSO.

Jones, R. (2006) (10th edn) *The Mental Health Act Manual*. London: Sweet and Maxwell.

Jordan, B. (1979) *Helping in Social Work*. London: Routledge and Kegan Paul.

Kadushin, A. (1992) (3rd. edn) *Supervision in Social Work*. New York: Columbia University Press.

Kagan, S. L. and Neville, P. R. (1993) *Integrating Services for Children and Families: Understanding the Past to Shape the Future*. New Haven: Yale University Press.

Katz, D. and Kahn, R. L. (1978) *The Social Psychology of Organizations*. New York: John Wiley.

Kelly, M. and Gamble, C. (2005) Exploring the concept of recovery in schizophrenia. *Journal of Psychiatric and Mental Health Nursing*, 12 (2), 245–51.

Kelly, S., Hill, S., Boardman, H. and Overton, I. (2004) Therapeutic communities. In Campling, P., Davies, S. and Faquaharson, G. (Eds) *From Toxic Institutions to Therapeutic Environments: Residential Settings in Mental Health Services*. London: RCP.

Kessler, R. C., Mickelson, K. D. and Williams, D. R. (1999) The prevalence, distribution, and mental health correlates of perceived discrimination in the United States. *Journal of Health and Social Behavior*, 40 (3), 208–30.

Kharicha, K., Levin, E., Iliffe, S. and Davies, B. (2004) Social work, general practice and evidence-based policy in the collaborative care of older people: current problems and future possibilities. *Health and Social Care in the Community*, 12 (2), 134–41.

King's Fund (2006) *Partnerships and Integration*. Reading list available at: www.kingsfund.org.uk/library

Kirsh, I., Deacon, B. J., Huedo-Medina, T. J., Scoboria, A., Moore, T. J. and Johnson, B. T. (2008) *Initial severity and antidepressant benefits: a meta-analysis of data submitted to the Food and Drug Administration PLoS Medicine*, 5 (2), e45. Available at: http://medicine.plosjournals.org

Kotsiubinskii, A. P. (2002) A biopsychosocial model of schizophrenia. *International Journal of Mental Health*, 31 (3), 51–60.

Kotter, J. (1995) leading change: why transformation efforts fail. *Harvard Business Review*, March–April.

Laing, R. D. (1960) *The Divided Self*. London: Penguin Books.

Langham, M. (1993) The rise and fall of social work. In Clarke, J. (Ed.) *A Crisis in Care*. London: Sage.

Lauber, C., Nordt, C., Braunschweig, C. and Rössler, W. (2006) Do mental health professionals stigmatize their patients? *Acta Psychiatrica Scandinavica*, 113 (s429), 51–9.

Leucht, S., Wahlbeck, K., Hamann, J. and Kissling, W. (2003) New generation antipsychotics versus low-potency conventional antipsychotics: a systematic review and meta-analysis. *The Lancet*, 361 (9369), 1581–9.

Lightfoot, J. (1995) Identifying needs and setting priorities: issues of theory, policy and practice. *Health and Social Care in the Community*, 3, 105–14.

Lymbery, M. (2001) Social work at the crossroads. *British Journal of Social Work*, 31 (3), 369–84.

Mahler, J. and Tavano, S. (2001) *The Recovery Model: A Conceptual Framework and Implementation Plan*. Contra Costa County Mental Health Recovery Task Force, October 2001, 1–8. Available at: www.dmh.ca.gov/MHSOAC/

McGowen, K. R. and Hart, L. E. (1990) Still different after all these years: gender differences in professional identity formation. *Professional Psychology: Research and Practice*, 21, 118–23.

McLaren, N. (2007) *Humanizing Madness: Psychiatry and Cognitive Neurosciences*. Ann Arbor, MI: Future Psychiatry Press.

McLaren, N. (1998) A critical review of the biopsychosocial model. *Australian and New Zealand Journal of Psychiatry*, 32 (1), 86–92.

Martin, J. K., Pescosoludo, B. A. and Tuch, S. A. (2000) Of fear and loathing: the role of 'disturbing behavior,' labels, and causal attributions in shaping public attitudes toward people with mental illness. *Journal of Health and Social Behavior*, 41 (2), 208–23.

Mintzberg, H. (1989) *Mintzberg on Management: Inside our Strange World of Organisations*. Chicago: Free Press.

Mirowsky, J., and Ross, C. E. (1989). *Social Causes of Psychological Distress*. New York: Aldine de Gruyter.

Moreland, M. (2007) *Mental Health Service User Movement?* BBC Action Network, available at: http://www.bbc.co.uk/dna/actionnetwork/A19232705

Morgan, C., Dazzan, P., Jones, P., Harrison, G., Leff, J., Murray, R. and Fearon, P., on behalf of the ÆSOP Study Group (2006) First episode psychosis and ethnicity: initial findings from the ÆSOP study. *World Psychiatry*, 5 (1), 40–46.

Muijen, M. (2003) Foreword. In Gilbert, P. (2003) *The Value of Everything*. London: Russell House Publishing.

National Treatment Agency (2008) *Non Medical Prescribing, Patient Group Directions, and Minor Ailment Schemes in the Treatment of Drug Misusers*. Available at: www.nta.nhs.uk

NHS, LA Confederation, DWP and CSCI (2007) *Putting People First: A Shared Vision and Commitment to the Transformation of Adult Social Care*. Ministerial Concordant. London: TSO.

NIAAA (1996) *Project Match: Main Findings*. Washington: NIAAA.

NICE (2007) *Drug Misuse and Dependence: Clinical Guidelines on Drug Misuse and Dependence*. London: TSO.

NICE (2007) *Compact Guidance on Commissioning Voluntary Sector Services*. London: TSO.NIMHE (2006) *The Social Work Contribution to Mental Health Services: A Discussion Paper*. London: NIMHE.

NIMHE (2003) *Personality Disorder: No Longer a Diagnosis of Exclusion*. London: DOH/TSO.

NIMHE/SCMH (2004) *The Ten Essential Shared Capabilities: A Framework for the Whole of the Mental Health Workforce*. London: Department of Health.

Niemi, P. M. (1997) Medical students' professional identity: self-reflection during the pre-clinical years. *Medical Education*, 31, 400–15.

Norman, I. J. and Peck, E. (1999) Working together in adult community mental health services: an inter-professional dialogue. *Journal of Mental Health*, 8 (3), 217–30.

Parry Jones, B. and Soulsby, J. (2001) Needs-led assessment: the challenges and the reality. *Health and Social Care in the Community*, 9 (6), 414–28.

Payne, M. (2006) (2nd edn) *What is Professional Social Work?* Bristol: BASW/Policy Press.

Pearlin, L. I. (1989). The sociological study of stress. *Journal of Health and Social Behavior*, 30, 241–56.

Peck, E., Gulliver, P. and Towel, D. (2002) Information, consultation or control: user involvement in mental health services in England at the turn of the century. *Journal of Mental Health*, 11 (4), 441–51.

Peck, E. and Norman, I. J. (1999) Working together in adult community mental health services: exploring inter-professional role relations. *Journal of Mental Health*, 8 (3), 231–42.

Petch, A (2007) Integration or fragmentation? *Journal of Integrated Care*, 15 (2), 38.

Platt, Dame D. (2006) *The State of Social Care*. London: DOH/TSO.

Pollitt, C. (1990) Doing business in the temple? Managers and quality assurance in the public services. *Public Administration*, 68 (4), 435–52.

Powell, F. W. (2001) *The Politics of Social Work*. London: Sage.

Ralph, R. O., Lambert, D., Kidder, K. A., and Muskie, E. S. (2002) *The Recovery Perspective and Evidence Based Practice for People with Serious Mental Illness: A guideline developed for the behavioural health recovery management project*. Chicago: University of Chicago. Available at: bhrm.org/guidelines/mhguidelines.htm

Read, J. and Law, A. (1999) The relationship of casual beliefs and contact with users of mental health services to attitudes to the 'mentally ill'. *International Journal of Social Psychiatry*, 45 (3), 216–29.

Read, J., Mosher, L. J. and Bentall, R. (2004) *Models of Madness: Psychological, Social and Biological Approaches to Schizophrenia*. London: Brunner-Routledge.

Reiger, D. A. (2003) Mental disorder diagnostic theory and practical reality: an evolutionary perspective. *Health Affairs*, 22 (5), 21–7.

Rethink (2005) *Future Perfect: Mental Health Service Users Set Out a Vision for the 21st Century*. Available via Rethink (www.rethink.co.uk).

Richter, D. (1999) Chronic mental illness and the limits of the biopsychosocial model. *Medicine, Health Care and Philosophy*, 2 (1), 21–30.

Rogers, E. S., Chamberlin, J., Ellison, M. L. and Crean, T. (1997) A consumer constructed scale to measure empowerment among users of mental health services. *Psychiatric Services*, 48, 1042–7.

Ross, J. (2007) The future direction of social care in light of the white paper *Our Health, Our Care, Our Say*. *Journal of Care Services Management*, 1 (4), 381–8.

Rowden, R. (2005) *Obstacle Course. Community Care*. Available at: www.communitycare.co.uk

Royal College of Psychiatry, Care Services Improvement Partnership and Social Care Institute for Excellence (2007) *A Common Purpose: Recovery in Future Mental Health Services*. RCP/CSIP/SCIE Joint Position Paper.

Rutter, D., Manley, C., Weaver, T., Crawford, M. J. and Fulop, N. (2004) Patients or partners? Case studies of user involvement in the planning and delivery of adult mental health services in London. *Social Science and Medicine*, 58 (10), 1973–84.

Sage, J. (2006) Schizophrenia: 'the biggy in mental health'. *Nurse Prescribing*, 4 (12), 146–9.

Sainsbury Centre for Mental Health (2001) *The Capable Practitioner*. London: SCMHE.

Scott, W. R. (1992) *Organizations: Rational, Natural, and Open Systems*. New Jersey: Prentice Hall.

Scott, W. R. and Meyer, J. W. (1994) *Institutional Environments and Organizations: Structural Complexity and Individualism*. California: Sage.

Sheppard, M. (1990) *Mental Health: The Role of the Approved Social Worker*. Sheffield: Community Care/University of Sheffield Joint Unit for Social Services Research.

Skills for Health (2007) *National Occupational Standards for Mental Health*. Available at: www.skillsforhealth.org.uk

Smith, H. (1992) Quality in community care. *Journal of Mental Health*, 1 (3), 207–16.

Smith, M. (2001) Risk assessment in mental health social work. *Practice*, 13 (2), 21–30.

Social Care Institute for Excellence (2005) *Developing Social Care: The Current Position*. London: SCIE.

Social Exclusion Unit (2004) *Social Exclusion and Mental Health: Social Exclusion Unit Report*. London: ODPM.

Social Exclusion Taskforce (2007) *Context for Social Exclusion Work*. Available at: www.cabinetoffice.gov.uk/ social_exclusion_task_force/context

Social Perspectives Network (2007) *Whose Health, Whose Care, Whose Say*. Available at: www.spn.org.uk

Social Perspectives Network (2004) *Integration of Health and Social Care: Promoting Social Care Perspectives Within Integrated Mental Health Services*. SPN Paper 6.

Social Services Inspectorate (2004) *Treated as People*. London: TSO/DOH.

Stacey, R. (1996) *Strategic Management and Organizational Dynamics*. 2nd edn, London: Pitman.

Sullivan, W. P. (1997). A long and winding road: the process of recovery from severe mental illness. In Spaniol, L., Gagne, C. and Koehler, M. (Eds) *Psychological and Social Aspects of Psychiatric Disability*. Boston: Centre for Psychiatric Rehabilitation.

Szasz, T. S. (1972) *The Myth of Mental Illness*. St Albans: Granada.

Tajfel, H. and Turner, J. (2001) An integrative theory of inter-group conflict. In Thompson, N. (2001) (3rd edn) *Anti-Discriminatory Practice*. Basingstoke: Palgrave Macmillan.

Taylor, B. and Barling, J. (2004) Identifying sources and effects of carer fatigue and burnout for mental health nurses: a qualitative approach. *International Journal of Mental Health Nursing*, 13 (2), 117–25.

Tew, J. (2005a) (Ed.) *Social Perspectives in Mental Health: Developing Social Models to Understand and Work with Mental Distress*. London: Jessica Kingsley.

Tew, J. (2005b) Power relations, social order and mental distress. In Tew, J. (Ed.) *Social Perspectives in Mental Health*. London: Jessica Kingsley.

Tew, J. (2005c) Core themes in social perspectives. In Tew, J. (Ed.) *Social Perspectives in Mental Health*. London: Jessica Kingsley.

Tew, J. (2002) Going social: championing a holistic model of mental distress within professional education. *Social Work Education*, 21 (2), 143–56.

Thompson, J. D. (1967) *Organizations in Action*. New York: McGraw-Hill.

Thornicroft, G. (2006) *Shunned: Discrimination Against People with Mental Illness*. Oxford: Oxford University Press.

Todd, M. (2002) Organisational Cclture and decision making. In Young, A. P. and Cooke, M. (2002) *Managing and Implementing Decisions in Health Care*. Edinburgh and New York: Balliere Tindall/Royal College of Nursing.

TOPSS (2002) *National Occupational Standards for Social Work*. London: TOPSS.

Townsend, W. and Glasser, N. (2003). Recovery: the heart and soul of treatment. *Psychiatric Rehabilitation Journal*, 27 (1), 83–6.

Truman, C. and Raine, P. (2002) Experience and meaning of user involvement: some explorations from a community mental health project. *Health and Social Care in the Community*, 10 (3), 136–43.

Tuunainen, A., Wahlbeck, K., and Gilbody, S. M. (2000) Newer atypical anti-psychotic medication versus clozapine for schizophrenia. Cochrane Database, available at: http://www.mrw.interscience.wiley.com/cochrane/cochrane_clsysrev_articles_fs.html

Vindlacheruvu, M. and Luxton, T. (2006) NHS continuing care: reliable decisions? *Age and Ageing*, 35, 313–16.

Wade, D. T.and Halligan. P. W (2004) Do biomedical models of illness make for good healthcare systems? *British Medical Journal*, 329, 1398–1401.

Wahlbeck, K., Cheine, M., and Essali, A., (1999) Evidence of clozapine's effectiveness in schizophrenia: a systematic review and meta-analysis of randomized trials. *American Journal of Psychiatry*, 156, 990–9.

Walton, P. (2000) Reforming the Mental Health Act 1983: an approved social worker perspective. *Journal of Social Welfare and Family Law*, 22 (4), 401–14.

Watts, T. (2007) *ADSS Advisory Paper on Mental Health Foundation Trusts*. Association of Directors of Social Services. Available at: www.integratedcarenetwork.gov.uk

Weick, K. E. and Quinn, R. E. (1999) Organisational change and development. *Annual Review of Psychology*, 50, 361–86.

Weinstein, J., Whittington, C., and Leiba, T. (2003) *Collaboration in Social Work Practice*. London: Jessica Kingsley.

Wethington, E. and Kessler, R. C. (1986). Perceived support, received support, and adjustment to stressful life events. *Journal of Health and Social Behavior*, 27, 78–89.

WHO (1993) *The ICD-10 Classification of Mental and Behavioural Disorders: Diagnostic Criteria for Research*. Geneva: WHO.

Williams, D. R. (1990). Socioeconomic differentials in health: A review and redirection. *Social Psychology Quarterly*, 53, 81–99.

Wilson, B. (1957). *Alcoholics Anonymous Comes of Age*. New York: Alcoholics Anonymous World Service.

Wistow, G. (2005) *Developing Social Care: Past, Present, and Future*. SCIE: London.

World Health Organisation (1998) *Health Promotion Glossary*. Geneva: WHO.

World Health Organisation (1993) *The Icd-10 Classification of Mental and Behavioural Diseases*. Switzerland: WHO.

Young, S. L. and Ensing, D. S. (1999) Exploring recovery from the perspective of people with psychiatric disabilities. *Psychiatric Rehabilitation Journal*, 22 (3), 219–31.

Young, A. and Ashton, E. (1956) *British Social Work in the Nineteenth Century*. London: Routledge and Kegan Paul.

Legislation/Acts of Parliament

National Assistance Act 1948

Mental Health Act 1983

NHS and Community Care Act 1990

Health Act 1999

Care Standards Act 2000

Mental Capacity Act 2005

NHS Act 2006

Mental Health (Amendment) Act 2007

Glossary

Acquisitive crime   Crime committed for the purposes of securing finances, usually an offence such as shoplifting, theft and robbery.

Alternate Provider of Services model (APS)   A group of organisations or singular organisation created to provide a service that would normally be provided by general practitioners or the local primary care trust. A key model of service provision within Practice Based Commissioning initiatives.

AMHP *see* **Approved Mental Health Professional**

Anti-psychiatry   A movement that challenged the fundamental practices and theories of mainstream psychiatry. It gained increasing support during the 1960s, although many of the movement's claims have now been discredited. The central premise was that biological and medical application to distress and disorders of the mind was both inappropriate and a form of social control.

AOT *see* **Assertive Outreach Team**

Approved Mental Health Professional (AMHP)   A new role under the Mental Health (Amendment) Act 2007 which replaces that of the ASW. The AMHP has the same powers and duties as the ASW but is extended to include nursing, occupational therapy and psychology professionals who have undertaken the required specialist training. AMHPs remain appointed by and required to act on behalf of the local authority, with effect from October 2008.

Approved Social Worker (ASW)   Social work role defined under the Mental Health Act 1983. ASWs are social workers who have undertaken specialist training within mental health law, and who have been appointed by the local authority to undertake the assessment and application of the duties prescribed under the Mental Health Act for those service users whose health and safety is at risk or who pose a risk to others due to the nature and/or degree of their mental disorder.

APS *see* **Alternate Provider of Services model**

Assertive Outreach Team (AOT)   Teams established as a result of the National Service Framework for Mental Health. The model of treatment differs from traditional mental health care delivery as it takes care to the patient, emphasises engagement and operates outside normal office hours. Usually the clients of the AOTs are chaotic mental health service users, often with a range of complex social and health-based problems.

ASW *see* **Approved Social Worker**

Biopsychosocial model   A model that posits that biological, psychological and social factors all play a significant role in human functioning in the context of disease or illness.

British Association of Social Work (BASW)   Professional body representing social work within the UK. Association membership is voluntary for qualified social workers.

CARAT *see* **Counselling, Assessment, Referral, Aftercare and Through care**

Care Programme Approach (CPA)   A standardised system of care management and care coordination, introduced in 1991, intended to be the basis for the care of people with mental health needs outside hospital. It applies to all people with serious mental health problems who are accepted as clients of specialist mental health services.

Care Services Improvement Partnership (CSIP)   Branch of the Department of Health established to provide good practice guidance and direction for service providers. Organised into regional centres and focusing on work streams aligned to the policy direction for service improvement.

Chaotic drug users (CDU)   Individuals who use substances (illicit and licit) to such an extent that their psychosocial functioning or health is severely affected.

CHC *see* **Continuing health care**

CJIT *see* **Criminal Justice Intervention Team**

CMHT *see* **Community Mental Health Team**

Commission for Social Care Inspection (CSCI)   Established in 2003 under the Care Standards Act 2000 and the Health and Social Care Act 2001, CSCI replaced the Social Services Inspectorate (SSI). CSCI is an independent body with a remit to monitor, regulate and inspect social care services.

Commissioning   The process of identifying a community's social and/or health care needs and finding services to meet them; the process of re-directing and allocating resources, according to agreed priorities.

Community Mental Health Team (CMHT)   Multi-disciplinary team of professionals operating within specified geographical areas, providing support to those with mental health problems living within the community.

Community psychiatric nurse (CPN)   Nursing professional trained in mental health care and operating within the community setting.

Community treatment order   A new order provided under the Mental Health (Amendment) Act 2007. Also know as supervised community treatment (SCT). Allows for formal powers to be applied to mental health patients within the community setting, including the application of treatment and the ability to specify certain conditions.

Continuing health care (CHC)   The eligibility framework against which service user needs are assessed, in order to determine whether the need is a primary health care one, and as such requires NHS funding.

Core Standards – Standards for Better Health   Suite of indicators developed and used by the Health Care Commission, against which health care services are inspected and regulated.

Counselling, Assessment, Referral, Aftercare and Through care (CARAT)   Substance misuse workers and teams based within the prison system, focused on short-term assessment and brief interventions, with a particular emphasis on onward referral to community-based services on release.

CPA *see* **Care Programme Approach**

CPN *see* **Community psychiatric nurse**

Criminal Justice Intervention Team (CJIT)   Services providing a comprehensive, holistic service to substance-misusing clients who are involved with the criminal justice system.

CSCI *see* **Commission for Social Care Inspection**

CSIP *see* **Care Services Improvement Partnership**

DAT/DAAT *see* **Drug Action Team/Drug and Alcohol Action Team**

Diagnostic and Statistical Manual of Mental Disorders (DSM)   American Handbook for Mental Health Professionals, listing categories of mental disorders and the associated symptoms to aid diagnosis.

DIP *see* **Drug Intervention Programme**

DRR *see* **Drug Rehabilitation Requirement**

Drug Action Team/Drug and Alcohol Action Team (DAT/DAAT)

Commissioning body for substance misuse services; each geographical area has its own DAAT/DAT, usually part of either the primary care trust or the local authority.

Drug Intervention Programme (DIP)   A criminal justice initiative that focuses on providing treatment to problematic drug users. The service is designed to engage with the broad range of drug-misusing offenders, who are at different stages in their drug misuse and offending careers. It aims to prevent crime through early interventions as well as to reduce crime levels by engaging the most problematic and prolific offenders.

Drug Rehabilitation Requirement (DRR)   A criminal justice community probation order placed upon offenders with drug misuse issues. Individual usually have requirements placed upon them to enter treatment and to submit to regular drug testing. Replaced the DTTO.

Drug Treatment and Testing Order (DTTO)   Precursor to the DRR: offenders were required to engage in treatment programmes which required up to 20 hours' contact per week, and included psychosocial intervention, substitute prescribing, social skills and leisure activities.

DSM *see* **Diagnostic and Statistical Manual of Mental Disorders**

DTTO *see* **Drug Treatment and Testing Order**

Eligibility criteria   A set of stated criteria by which an authority or organisation makes a decision in regards to providing or not providing care of services.

Essential Shared Capabilities (ESC)   Suite of competencies defined by the National Institute for Mental Health (NIMH) and the Sainsbury Centre for Mental Health (SCMH) as a framework for the mental health workforce.

Fair Access to Care (FAC)   The eligibility framework against which service user needs are assessed, in order to determine whether the need is a primary social care one, and as such requires local authority funding.

General Social Care Council (GSCC)   The registration and professional body for social workers and social care workers.

Glasgow formula   Developed by Glasgow University, this statistical formula is used to estimate the number of chaotic drug users in a given catchment area, using a range of demographic and socio-economic data.

Health Act flexibilities   Introduced by the Health Act 1999 (superseded by the NHS Act 2006), allowing health and social services authorities to form a range of partnership arrangements to improve and streamline the provision of services.

Health Care Commission (HCC)   The independent inspection body for both the NHS and independent health care. Undertakes inspections, reviews and surveys of staff and service users to ascertain and promote quality standards in the delivery of all aspects of health care.

Integrated Care Network (ICN)   A division of CSIP, focusing on the issues arising from integrating health and social care and promoting good practice in the field.

International Classification of Diseases (ICD)   Published by the World Health Organisation (WHO), a section of which is dedicated to the classification and diagnostic criteria associated with the whole range of identified mental disorders.

Mental Health Act Commission   Regulatory body for the use of powers under the Mental Health Act 1983 (and subsequently the Mental Health (Amendment) Act 2007.

Mental Health National Occupational Standards (MHNOS)

A framework of 96 standards which set out the competencies required of workers within the mental health field. Defined by Skills for Care, these standards related to the NHS knowledge and skills framework and are designed to promote evidence-based capable practice within the delivery of mental health care.

National Service Framework (NSF)   Policy document and initiative that provides a systematic approach with which to tackle the agenda of improving standards and quality across health care sectors. NSFs are implemented in partnership with social care and other organisations.

National Treatment Agency (NTA)   A specialist department of the Department of Health which governs the provision of drug treatment services across England and Wales.

Nearest relative   A relative of the service user defined within the Mental Health Act 1983 (s 26). This is a legal term and is not necessarily the same person as the individual's stated next of kin. The law provides a hierarchy of relatives, based upon blood relation and age.

NSF *see* **National Service Framework**

NTA *see* **National Treatment Agency**

PCT *see* **Primary Care Trust**

Performance assessment framework (PAF)   A suite of key performance indicators used by CSCI to assess the quality and performance of social services authorities and their partners.

Practice Based Commissioning   is a government policy which devolves responsibility for commissioning services from Primary Care Trusts (PCTs) to local GP practices. Under Practice Based Commissioning, practices are be given a commissioning budget which they will have the responsibility for using in order to provide services.

Primary Care Trust (PCT)   An NHS commissioning authority. Some PCTs also have a provider arm, but the focus on commissioning services and developing strategic direction is the responsibility of all PCTs for the areas they serve.

Procurement   The acquisition of goods or services at the best possible cost, in the right quantity and quality, at the right time, in the right place for the direct benefit or use of governments, corporations, or individuals, generally via a contract.

Responsible clinician (RC)   A new role defined under the Mental Health (Amendment) Act 2007, which replaces the previous role of responsible medical officer. The RC acts as the responsible professional overseeing the care of a patient subject to formal requirements under the Mental Health Act.

SET *see* **Social Exclusion Taskforce**

SEU *see* **Social Exclusion Unit**

Single point of contact (SPOC)   A recognised and publicised access point which can facilitate service users' contact with the full range of health and social care services.

Social enterprise   Local community or community organisations, acting together to provide services needed by the local population, particularly where the service cannot be provided through the market economy.

Social Exclusion Taskforce (SET)   Established in June 2006, its aim is to extend the opportunities enjoyed by the vast majority of people in the UK to those whose lives have been characterised by deprivation and exclusion.

Social Exclusion Unit (SEU)   A division of the Cabinet Office established to look at issues of social exclusion. The unit was disbanded in 2006 and replaced by the Social Exclusion Taskforce.

SPOC *see* **Single point of contact**

Substitute prescribing   A prescribing regime designed to replace a dependence on illicit substances. In the case of heroin, methadone or buprenorphine are the most common regimes that are introduced. These drugs minimise the physical dependence upon illicit substances and allow the user time and stability in order to address social and behavioural issues.

Support, Time and Recovery (STR) Worker   Support worker, dedicated to the service user in terms of time and intensive social support, aiming to promote social inclusion and daily living skills as part of an overall care package.

Tiers 1–4: Substance misuse services   Tiers of substance misuse treatment, set out in the *Models of Care* framework, which service users move through as they undertake the treatment journey.

Tier 1 – information and signposting services;

Tier 2 – open access, needle exchanges, drop-in services;

Tier 3 – structured treatment, substitute prescribing and psychosocial interventions;

Tier 4 – residential detoxification and rehabilitation services.

Index